Executive Team Leadership in the Global Economic and Competitive Environment

T0265194

Corporations have continued to grow and extend their operations into the global economy to the point that the modern corporation has become larger and more influential than many sovereign countries. In this global expansion, corporations have extended their operations with little restraint—almost only limited by corporate lawyers' imaginations. Modern corporations have become so pervasive that world populations are more dependent on them for their food, services, technologies, work, and daily well-being than ever before.

This book analyzes the twenty-first-century forces challenging the executive leadership of the modern corporation. Lessons are drawn for corporate leaders facing these challenges: turbulent times, balancing creators and stewards, managing company culture, managing by wire, incorporating global virtual organization structures, and managing sustained innovation. Nolan concludes with guidelines on creating a leadership agenda for transforming the corporation to successfully compete in the realities of the new corporate world of the twenty-first century.

Richard L. Nolan is the William Barclay Harding Endowed Professor of Business Administration, Emeritus at Harvard Business School, United States. He was the first recipient of the Boeing Philip M. Condit Endowed Professor of Business Administration at the Foster School of Business Administration, University of Washington in 2003, and in 2012, he became Professor Emeritus.

Routledge Studies in Leadership Research

Executive Team Leadership in the Global Economic and Competitive Environment

Richard L. Nolan

Routledge
Taylor & Francis Group

LONDON AND NEW YORK

First published 2015
by Routledge

2 Park Square, Milton Park, Abingdon, Oxfordshire OX14 4RN
711 Third Avenue, New York, NY 10017

*Routledge is an imprint of the Taylor & Francis Group,
an informa business*

First issued in paperback 2018

Library of Congress Cataloging-in-Publication Data
CIP data for this book has been applied for.

ISBN: 978-1-138-81387-8 (hbk)
ISBN: 978-1-138-61707-0 (pbk)

Typeset in Sabon
by Apex CoVantage, LLC

To all the many people who have generously shared their experiences and insights with me and from whom I learned so much about the exciting and important corporate journey into the twenty-first century—and a special thanks to the people of the Boeing Corporation who I have had the pleasure of working with and knowing throughout my working and academic career.

Contents

Figures and Tables

FIGURES

TABLES

Foreword

In *Executive Team Leadership in the Global Economic and Competitive Environment,* Dick Nolan writes about nothing less than the struggle between twentieth-century leadership, well established and familiar, and twenty-first-century leadership, emerging, better, but struggling to gain credibility. Most important, he's showing us what twenty-first-century leadership ought to be.

Dick explores the tension between twenty-first-century and twentieth-century leadership by taking an in-depth look at the 787 Dreamliner project at Boeing. It's not an account that everyone at Boeing, especially some executive leaders, will embrace. As I read it, this book presents the story of a company working hard to reinvent itself and, in the process, trying to move toward a new and better form of executive leadership. The 787 project was bold, as were the original ideas about how to execute it. Boeing aimed to create not only a new kind of airplane but also a new kind of company.

But, alas, change is difficult, and old leadership styles die hard. Moreover, making airplanes is an expensive and unforgiving business. Airplanes carry precious cargo in extreme conditions, for decades, and cannot be allowed to ever fail. And the 787 project stretched out over many years, plenty of time for ideas to lose momentum or to be second guessed, time for leaders, and their philosophies of leadership, to change, for better and worse. Although some of the words on the pages that follow could be interpreted as critical of the company's leaders, the overall treatment is fair and sympathetic. Dick Nolan started his career at Boeing, and he has traveled alongside the company for decades as an advisor and executive development mentor. It's abundantly clear that he cares about Boeing, its products, and its people, and this stance adds immensely to the penetrating nature of his insights.

In so many ways, Dick is exactly the right person to tell this story. You can read his full bio elsewhere in this book, but it's worth pausing to consider the experience Dick brings to the ambitious task of creating fresh ideas about leadership: "whiz kid" in the McNamara Pentagon; Harvard Business School professor; author of numerous highly influential business books and papers; intellectual progenitor of the stages and maturity models widely used in the IT and other industries; a pioneer of the consulting business

Nolan, Norton & Co., which Dick co-founded and ran with David Norton until they sold it to KPMG in 1987, and which has served as a prototype for dozens of today's top management consulting firms. In my own travels in the business world, it sometimes seems that almost everyone in a senior position has worked for Dick at some point, or has at least turned to him for advice.

I've had the great honor of working closely with Dick since about 1997. In this time, I have never had a conversation with him that did not yield new insights. He's the epitome of a big idea guy. His thoughts lead to non-intuitive places. And he is right scandalously often. After working with Dick for only a couple of years, I decided he was the one person in the world whom I would bet *with* even if I thought he was wrong. Because I have, as a rule, more faith in the insightfulness of his views than in any amount of my own analysis.

In the end, this book and its conclusions reach far beyond any single company. The book calls on us to develop the practice of executive team leadership to a new level and includes the ideas to help us do it. As he relates this story about one company, Dick also unfolds a comprehensive system of thought that he has developed and evolved throughout his rich and varied career. Some of the themes are familiar from his past work: how IT continues to transform how companies are organized and how they manage their work, the power of strategic partnerships and ecosystems, "integration" as a vital management skill, the importance of "creators" and how they could be managed. In bringing it all together, he helps us see clearly why twenty-first-century leadership is inadequate for twenty-first-century challenges and shows us the emerging and more promising contributions of twenty-first-century management.

In the time that I have worked with him, Dick has often repeated an interesting phrase: "To go to the future, you must live in the future." Dick has always lived in the future. Not very many people can do this. Most of us eventually grasp tightly onto the old and the familiar. We want to think that what has worked for us before, which we know so well, will work again tomorrow. In this book, Dick Nolan shows us that this is not true. The future is coming, whether we like it or not, and it is different, in important ways, from the past. Let us hope we can shake off old reflexes and abandon old comforts. If we can do it, we can leverage the contents of this important book into a new form of leadership practice, a form that can help us solve the world's grand challenges and seize its grand opportunities. As Hemingway once said, "The world is a fine place and well worth fighting for." If we are wise enough to see it, Dick has equipped us here for the fight.

Robert D. Austin, Professor, Management of Creativity and Innovation, Copenhagen Business School.

Preface

Executive Team Leadership in the Global Economic and Competitive Environment is a result of firsthand experience, extensive case research, and an extended study of successful twentieth-century corporations striving to maintain success in the twenty-first century, along with the newer corporations founded by entrepreneurial digital natives at the dawn of the new century. Both the old guard and the new pioneers offer critical insights about achieving corporate success in changing times.

The twentieth century was a time of founding, learning, and growth of corporations as they became the majority of the largest organizations in the world. The breakthroughs in national economic well-being during that time arose in no small part from the advent of innovative factory work and mass production. Successful twenty-first-century corporations are going beyond twentieth-century corporations in learning to extend their organizations to tap into the global workforce and leverage IT investments to serve global customers. These corporations are not doing it in the old way of steady growth and punctuated innovations. Instead, these new corporate forms operate at close to the speed of light, analyze big data, and sense and respond in getting it right. They don't read reports to discover what is happening, they *know* what's happening and act. They opportunistically extend their organizations through virtual integration with global partners.

Using old twentieth-century terms like "outsourcing" to describe these new extended virtual organizations misses the essence of these new forms and muddles understanding of what the new forms are all about.

More than ever before, CEO leaders and their executive teams need to become intense serial/real-time learners, absorbing the incessant innovations and inventing new ways to shape and transform their corporations for this fast-moving environment. It is not a quick learn. It takes a thorough grounding in present developments, supported by a broad understanding of both the greenfield creation of successful twenty-first-century corporations and the difficult transformation of twentieth-century corporations into successful twenty-first-century corporations. My objective for this book is to provide that foundational grounding, using key real-world examples, to offer a starting point for twenty-first-century executives.[1]

Global information technology has accelerated the pace of business the way jet propulsion accelerated air travel. The innovations are nonstop. The half-life of learnings is a few years, rapidly replaced by new thinking and discovery.

I got my start on this project after fourteen years of consulting with major corporations on strategic use of IT and upon selling Nolan, Norton and Company to KPMG. I then returned to the Harvard Business School faculty. I knew something important was going on with corporations, and I wanted to research and learn more about it. During this time, I continued to build a foundation of published books, articles, and personal interviews with a diverse group of executive leaders.[2]

The idea for this book originated in a 2003 conversation with then Boeing CEO and Chairman, Phil Condit, who, together with the Dean of the University of Washington's Foster Business School and the President of the University, asked me to accept the new Philip M. Condit chaired professorship at the business school. I was especially intrigued by my discussions with Phil Condit about Boeing's "large systems integrator" strategy, its transformation into the twenty-first century, and the rather extraordinary number of highly successful innovative companies located in the Puget Sound region. I accepted the Condit chair, which also involved chairing the University of Washington/Boeing fast-track management development (AIMS) program, which I did for five years. During this time I got reacquainted with the senior management team along with many of their promising management and engineering professionals. I led groups of participants in projects at a number of the Boeing factories and research facilities. I concluded that the study of the Boeing Corporation's growth and transformation initiative provided a generalizable case on executive leadership into the twenty-first-century global environment.

Professor Suresh Kotha, a colleague from the Foster School of Business at the University of Washington who also served as a member of our AIMS faculty team, and I researched and conducted interviews on Boeing's new 787 airplane program, and co-authored a case titled "Boeing 787: Dreamliner."[3] We taught the Boeing Dreamliner case during the five years that I chaired the AIMS program, and a diverse set of Boeing managers continued to provide us insights on the Dreamliner product-driven transformation and its execution.

By 2009, my outline for the proposed book took form. I explained my objectives to Phil Condit, and he agreed to review my chapter drafts and share his perspectives on "being there" and as a subject matter expert. More importantly, Phil impressed on me the importance of CEO leadership of global corporations, their importance, and the real challenges of complexity in the new century. He said that he faced critical challenges in leading and transforming Boeing into the twenty-first century and that he anxiously embraced the idea of an informed academic's perspective and third-party observations and opinions.

We engaged in hours of video interviews both in person and via Skype. During these conversations, I learned more about the nature of the Boeing CEOs; their leadership; and the important role that company culture played in obtaining, losing, regaining, and sustaining Boeing's industry leadership for more than fifty years. Once having grounded my research in an extended case study of Boeing, I expanded my inquiries to include cases of other corporations in various stages of transformation to the twenty-first-century environment. These cases included Otis Elevator, Cisco Systems, IBM, Apple, Amazon, and Google.

These cases underscored another important research study that we conducted on the long-run collaboration among a diverse group of university researchers and companies that created the Internet. The kind of vision and execution that built the Internet provided insights to the workings of twentieth-century corporations in coordinating global activities as they create exceedingly complex products and services.

NOTES

1. The foundation for developing this book includes several previous works. For functional management and business operations leaders, we have published a book on mastery of critical skills toward becoming a twenty-first-century executive: Austin, Nolan, and O'Donnell, *Adventures of an IT Leader* (Boston: Harvard Business Press, 2009); for CEOs and their executive teams, we have published a second book on the leadership journey: Austin, Nolan, and O'Donnell, *Harder Than I Thought* (Boston: Harvard Business Press, 2013).
2. These publications include Nolan and Croson, *Creative Destruction* published by Harvard Business Press, 1995; Haeckel and Nolan, "Management by Wire" published by *Harvard Business Review*, September–October 1993, and Austin and Nolan, "Stewards and Creators" *Sloan Management Review*, Winter 2007.
3. Boeing 787: Dreamliner, HBS case #9–305–101. Revised June 21, 2005.

Acknowledgments

I have conducted extensive interviews with numerous people in conducting the research for this book. I have received advice and insights from colleagues at the Harvard Business School, the University of Washington, and many Boeing executives and previous Boeing employees, along with many other people from other successful corporations. Unfortunately, it is impossible to thank all of them here in the limited space of acknowledgments. But for those who read these words, please know how grateful I am for your help in so many ways.

I owe a debt of gratitude to the many executives participating in our AIMS Executive Education classes—both as students and as guest speakers. I owe a special debt of gratitude to Phil Condit, during whose tenure as Boeing CEO (1996–2003) the Boeing 2016 transformation vision was created, and the 787 program was conceptualized and launched. During the summer of 2009, I contacted Phil Condit by letter about developing the Boeing case into an extended case on the evolution of the modern corporation and CEO leadership. Phil agreed to review my early draft chapters and discuss them with me through a series of video interviews.

In regard to his own CEO leadership, Phil Condit emphasized that he wanted me to remain an objective third party in my analysis and conclusions. And in the interest of full disclosure, it is important to state that the Boeing endowment partially covered some of my expenses in conducting the interviews and expenses of the Boeing case research.

I thank the numerous 787 program leaders: Steve Westby, Bob Noble, Scott Strode, Ross Bogue, and many other managers and engineers who discussed various aspects of the program with me. My special thanks to Mike Bair, the first project leader of the 787 program, who provided an overall strategic perspective on the many innovations involved in the program and how Boeing created such a complex product.

Also, special thanks to Joe Sutter, a legendary Boeing aeronautical engineer, and retired chief engineer of the 747 program. Joe provided perspective on Boeing's approach to technology, innovation, and manufacturing risk management. He maintained an office at Boeing Renton, where he held frequent conversations with the 787 program engineers and management team.

I owe a very deep debt to Colleen Kaftan, my development editor, who has worked tirelessly with me through the drafts of this book, helping me to develop and tease out the critical ideas of twenty-first-century corporate leadership. Colleen was adamant in ensuring that information and research was on point and concise in explicating the main themes of the book.

Finally, I thank the deans of the Harvard Business School and University of Washington Foster School of Business, who encouraged me and provided financial support for the research and writing of this book. Four Harvard Business School deans supported my work through their tenures: Dean John MacArthur, Dean Kim Clark, Dean Jay Light, and Dean Nitin Nohria. Three Foster School of Business deans at the University of Washington supported my work through their tenures: Dean Yash Gupta, Acting Dean David Burgstahler, and Dean Jim Jiambalvo. In addition, Associate Dean Tom Lee was a valued mentor to me and supporter of the work, including reading and commenting on the developing book chapter drafts, as well as reviewing associated journal articles and case studies.

Richard L. Nolan, 2015

1 Turbulent Times

A chorus of thousands roared, "Touchdown!" These euphoric observers were cheering not at an athletic event, but for Chief Pilot Mike Carriker's perfect maiden flight of the Boeing 787 Dreamliner. All over the world, people watching on television and the Internet were applauding as well. There were many issues still to address, but if successful, the 787 would become the fourth industry game-changing commercial airliner[1] built by the venerable Boeing Corporation.

The long-awaited touchdown set off delayed celebration parties across the globe. More than a few of the revelers had despaired of ever seeing the revolutionary aircraft get off the ground. Designed in collaboration with Boeing's airline customers and a global outsourcing team, the Dreamliner was a medium-sized, very high-tech plane efficient enough to be economical in flying long hauls point to point. It could thereby challenge the prevailing hub-and-spoke industry structure, in which commuter and smaller airplanes brought passengers to a hub airport, where they boarded big commercial airplanes to fly long distances. The Dreamliner represented bold changes not only in the composite materials it was made of, but also in the way it would be manufactured.

Still, critics remained skeptical about its chances for commercial success. Boeing was suffering from turbulent times, and launching the 787 offered the best hope for salvation. But with more than three and a half years of delivery delays and penalty costs surpassing $20 billion, one of America's best-known corporations was struggling to regain its fragile viability.

The delays were embarrassing, the subject of widespread speculation and derision in global financial markets. On July 8, 2007 (7/8/7) the first 787 was rolled out on live TV, with Tom Brokaw hosting a special Today Show broadcast.[2] The first 787 flight had been scheduled for the second quarter (April–June) 2008, and the first delivery during fourth quarter 2008.[3]

Little known to the world but well known to the Boeing workers at the time, the 2007 rollout was for show purposes only, the flight and delivery dates as much a dream as the aircraft itself. The prototype was far from complete, and, as rumor had it, "cabled together with baling wire." It had arrived in pieces aboard a giant, specially fitted-out 747 "Dreamlifter" that landed at the Boeing Everett final assembly factory on April 24, 2007, to be "clicked" together into the rollout Dreamliner 787.[4] The Dreamlifter was an innovative part of the 787 new airplane program, enabling breakthrough efficiencies in integrating a network of global partners from all over North America, Southeast Asia, and Europe. But Boeing's global partners and suppliers had delivered the major components in various states of completion, several of them falling far short of specifications. The 787 program was in serious trouble, but Boeing kept that information under wraps for more than a year after the rollout.

The business processes for the 787 program differed dramatically from Boeing's twentieth-century "build to print" processes. The conventional processes for previous aircraft programs began with a relatively small team of one to two hundred to participate in conceptual design. This team would then convene Boeing contractors and suppliers for further conceptual design of the new airplane. Once the conceptual design of the airplane was agreed upon, the design-engineering group exploded to thousands, who would engage in detailed design and development of detailed engineering drawings, which eventually would be fanned out to Boeing manufacturing facilities and contract suppliers. If a supplier subsequently ran into problems, Boeing sent out teams to help the supplier get back on track, working from the detailed engineering drawings.

The 787 program deviated from this process.[5] Instead of "build to print," a group of Tier 1 partners would be chosen to "build to performance"—that is, performance specifications would be supplied by Boeing to Tier 1 partners, and Tier 1 partners would develop detailed drawings from which to build the major components of the airplane. Global partners would create their own tooling to build the major sections for the finished components—that is, a Tier 1 component would be fully completed including electrical systems, fuel tanks, and the like, so final assembly could be simplified and shortened to mere days. All partners would use an extremely sophisticated IT-based CAD/CAM system, centrally coordinated by Boeing to ensure that all the Tier 1 parts came together into "fully stuffed" major components ready to be "clicked" together during final assembly.

Boeing selected thirty Tier 1 global strategic partners, and their engineering teams came to Seattle to do preliminary engineering design. These partners represented the most diverse global talent pool ever assembled to create a Boeing new commercial airplane. They were assigned to eight teams: (1) fuselage; (2) propulsion; (3) services; (4) interiors; (5) systems; (6) production; (7) integration; and (8) wing, empennage (i.e., an aviation term for the airplane tail section), and landing gear.[6]

The Boeing 787 would be the most outsourced commercial airplane ever built, with approximately 35 percent main Tier 1 integrated components built by Boeing, and the rest outsourced among fifteen companies residing in ten countries: the United States, Japan, England, Italy, Canada, China, South Korea, Australia, and Sweden. The main Boeing control point was at the

Tier 1 level with successively lower tiers (Tiers 2, 3, and 4) largely delegated through the supply chain companies all the way down to elementary parts such as fasteners (parts that connect the pieces of an airplane together such as rivets, screws, adhesives, etc.).

The global scope and coordination/management challenges of the program were daunting:

- The two "quick change" interchangeable engines were designed and built by GE (United States) and Rolls Royce (United Kingdom).
- The fuselage sections were built in the United States (forward fuselage—Spirit Aerosystems) and rear fuselage sections—Vought), Japan (mid-fuselage section—Kawasaki Heavy Industries), and Italy (mid-fuselage sections—Alenia Aeronautica).
- Wings were built in Japan by Mitsubishi Heavy Industries with moveable trailing edges built by Boeing Australia and the fixed and leading moving edges built by Boeing.[7]
- Other major parts were outsourced to be integrated during final assembly, which included the landing gear (United Kingdom), entry doors (France), engine nacelles (Canada), wing tips (Korea), rudder (China), tail fin (United States), horizontal stabilizer (Italy), and cargo access doors (Sweden).
- A number of highly integrated systems were coordinated by outsources: Japanese and French entities coordinated the in-flight entertainment system; French outsourcers and Boeing US coordinated the inside cockpit avionics, internal electrical power, and electric controls and components.
- Final assembly was conducted in the Boeing Everett plant and the newly constructed Boeing South Carolina Charleston plant.

To facilitate coordination among Boeing and its thirty Tier 1 outsourcing partners, Boeing contracted with IBM and Dassault Systemes S.A. to develop one of the most sophisticated Project Lifecycle Management (PLM)/CAD/CAM systems. Boeing also built a state-of-the-art command and control center (equipped with video conferencing and high data transmission speeds) that allowed all partners to share and coordinate using the same CAD/CAM drawings of the 787 airplane. This Puget Sound center would operate 24/7, 365 days a year, to work and coordinate with Boeing's global outsourcing partners. In addition, Boeing deployed its own engineers to each of their Tier 1 sites to facilitate on-site communications and coordination. And despite all of this sophisticated expertise and coordination, the Dreamliner program repeatedly flirted with disaster.

The saga of the Dreamliner illustrates the kind of twenty-first century leadership dramas taking place every day in other established corporations. Boeing's troubled 787 program experience serves as a cautionary tale to help other firms avoid similar pitfalls. Two overarching questions lead to critical insights for all managers. First, what went wrong? How did things get so out of hand to deal a near-fatal blow to such a successful and important corporation? Second, and equally important, what went right? How did Boeing go on to build the industry game-changing, most technologically advanced commercial airplane ever, and price it at the time about the same as its thirty-year-old 767?

As the Boeing dignitaries congratulated the test pilots after the maiden flight, a veteran mechanic blurted out the beginning of an answer to both questions: "It flew because we made it fly." The mechanic spoke of Boeing's company culture, shaped by founder Bill Boeing and further developed under successive Boeing CEOs to become one of the corporation's most important assets. Company culture is a term and subject that has been in vogue at business schools and in the popular press in the twenty-first century. Yet company culture deeply influenced corporate performance all through the twentieth century, as well.

Two key tenets described the Boeing culture: "Let no airplane technology pass us by" and "Build to perfection." The first underscores the technical advances in every generation of Boeing airplanes. The second reveals itself through the high reliability performance of the thousands of in-service Boeing airplanes continuously flying around the world. Every part of every airplane needs to do its job perfectly, and to work smoothly with every other part of the broader aviation system.

EVOLVING CORPORATE GROWTH AND COMPLEXITY

It often helps to consider a company's history in order to contemplate its future prospects. Founded in 1916, Boeing reached a modest $36 million in annual revenues by 1934, when it operated the third largest factory in the United States. It wasn't until 1954 that annual revenues broke the $1 billion mark, placing Boeing in a small group of twenty-two other U.S. companies with revenues at that level. Further organic growth brought Boeing's 1996 revenues to $37 billion. That same year, Boeing announced its newest CEO, Phil Condit, and Condit presented his team's bold 2016 strategy for maintaining Boeing's forty-plus years of aerospace industry leadership into the twenty-first century. The most striking departure from previous efforts entailed supplementing organic growth with targeted acquisitions in the space and defense sectors, including the 1997 purchase of competitor McDonnell-Douglas. Assimilating McDonnell-Douglas's annual revenues of $17 billion raised the combined company's total revenue to $54 billion and severely jolted Boeing, its culture, and its executive management team. It wasn't too long after the acquisition that some Boeing workers and the press started referring to the newly reorganized Boeing as "McBoeing," in reference to the acquired company's influence over the parent.[8] The challenges of managing far-flung strategic partners, a global supply chain, and multiple governmental relationships would knock the execution of the 787 program drastically off course.

The year 2003 brought another shock when Airbus passed Boeing in the number of commercial airliners sold and claimed the industry leader's position. Airbus also threatened to unseat Boeing's largest commercial airplane marquee: the Boeing 747, "queen of the skies." Plans for the giant, two-decker Airbus 380—the "king of the skies"—would dwarf Boeing's long-reigning queen, the B-747.

GAME OVER?

When the first set of outsourced Dreamliner components arrived at Boeing's final assembly plant far from finished and impossible to click together as planned to produce a finished 787 in three days, many thought "game over." Successfully completing the 787 program appeared nearly impossible. But then the exceptionally strong Boeing company culture clicked in. In short, the thousands of Boeing workers refused to let the 787 fail over program leadership shortcomings. Engineers and mechanics rallied together to propel the 787 program to the successful maiden flight, and, a year later, to full certification.

This remarkable recovery took place despite the CEO leadership team's decision to locate the second 787 final assembly line not adjacent to the first final assembly line in Everett, but rather at a brand new plant in South Carolina where newly recruited, nonunion employees would constitute the second line. Many long-term employees argued that this decision would deliver a weakening blow to an ill-understood but immensely valuable asset—the Boeing culture.

The Seattle-based Boeing culture's most distinctive element was not obvious until actually observed. It showed up in the way that the Boeing engineers worked hand in glove with test pilots and with the Boeing mechanics on the assembly line. It exuded a high level of mutual respect and give and take. It combined theory and practice and nearly a century of learning about building complex commercial airplanes by discovering and resolving problems during early manufacturing. Doing these things well was a significant determinant of profitability for the overall airplane program. Reproducing these learning processes in locations more than 3,000 miles apart with significantly different cultural antecedents would be difficult, to say the least.

Understanding how the 787 program went off course and then recovered—several times—requires a broader examination of Boeing's growth through the twentieth century and into the twenty-first. Boeing's experience parallels that of other venerable corporations as they have evolved from modest beginnings to become major players in the global economy.

FIVE STAGES OF TWENTIETH-CENTURY CORPORATE DEVELOPMENT

The modern corporation grew up in the twentieth century: childhood and adolescence in the first part, and young adulthood in the latter part. Boeing's history typifies the stages of evolution many other corporations shared during that time, as summarized in Figure 1.1, *Evolution of the Boeing Corporation.*

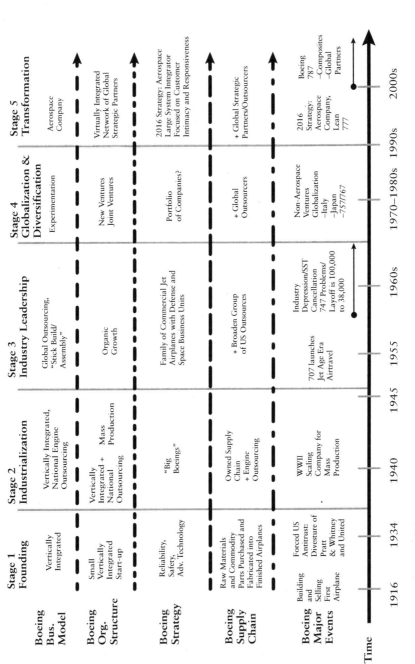

Figure 1.1 Evolution of the Boeing Corporation

Stage 1: Founding

As founder and chief architect of the first stage, Bill Boeing built and piloted the first Boeing airplane and then secured a profitable revenue stream flying mail and passengers. On March 3, 1919, Bill Boeing (Figure 1.2, standing left) and Eddie Hubbard flew the Boeing Model C from Vancouver, Canada, to Seattle—the first U.S. international airmail flight.

In 1933, Boeing introduced its first industry game-changing commercial airplane, the Boeing 247—an all-metal, low-wing, two-engine, passenger airplane with a range of 745 miles flying at more than 200 miles per hour. The Daniel Guggenheim Medal was established in 1929 for the purpose of honoring persons who make notable achievements in the advancement of aeronautics. It was sponsored by the The American Institute of Aeronautics and Astronautics.

The medal commemorated Bill Boeing's efforts in creating the vertically integrated United Aircraft and Transport Corporation, which combined the major business units of Boeing Manufacturing, Pratt-Whitney Aircraft Engines, and United Airlines. Boeing had built the leading company in a new industry that would continue to thrive well after his departure. And he had done so in an amazingly short eighteen years.

Figure 1.2 First U.S. International Airmail Flight

An antitrust action filed in 1934 brought Boeing to a critical juncture. The judgment required the company to divest its Pratt-Whitney and United Air Transport operations, both of which continued to thrive independently for years to come. At the same time, the brilliant and pioneering factory manager, P. G. Johnson (hired earlier from the University of Washington's fledgling engineering program), was forced to leave. Bill Boeing, now in his fifties, had already been planning his own exit strategy and was preparing to turn over the leadership to the talented young team he had mentored. The antitrust action accelerated his plan. He sold his stock and left the company he had built, disappointed by the ruling but confident that his hand-picked successors would manage his legacy well.

For the most part, Bill Boeing was right in assuming that the company would be in good hands with his successors—and, later, under the leaders they would recruit, nurture, and place in charge at key inflection points.

Frequently, when the founder leaves, the existing management team tries to continue exploiting (or "milk") the original successful product(s). The cash flow from an existing product line (even one that is approaching the end of its life) often obscures the need to invest in innovative newer products or services for future prosperity.

Fortunately for Boeing, the founder appointed Clairmont Egtvedt, head of the talented cadre of aeronautical design engineers that now formed the core of Boeing, to take over as president in 1933. Egtvedt and his team accomplished something that many young companies fail to do: they developed an innovative follow-on to Boeing's first product line and eventually transformed the organization in order to deliver it.

Egtvedt invested aggressively in his "big Boeings" strategy, beginning with a prototype that ultimately became the B-17. Its development costs almost bankrupted Boeing, but the company was saved when the United States was drawn into World War II. Boeing won the B-17 production contract and entered into Stage 2 of company development: industrialization.

Stage 2: Industrialization

The Boeing Corporation moved to the next stage of market growth by introducing cost-efficient mass production techniques. It is a twentieth-century story repeated many times over across corporations in many industries. Boeing and other corporations mastered the process of mass production and mass distribution, thereby increasing revenues from millions of dollars to billions of dollars.

The production demands of WWII forced Boeing management to figure out how to mass produce B-17s at unprecedented rates. The board concluded that these demands would require a different kind of leader, and Egtvedt agreed to step down as president in 1939. He continued to serve as chairman of the board and also returned to his previous position as head of the engineering group.[9] The board lobbied successfully for permission to rehire P. G. Johnson, the manufacturing expert forced out by the antitrust ruling, and persuaded him to return as president in 1939.

Johnson and his team turned the Seattle Plant 2 factory into one of the most successful mass production facilities in the world. In one twenty-four-hour period in April 1944, the factory produced sixteen B-17s—a rate of large airplane production that has not since been matched. Unfortunately, while touring a Boeing plant toward the end of WWII, Johnson suffered a severe stroke and passed away. In his place, the board named Bill Allen as the new CEO. Already a long-serving and valuable board member whose legal and management expertise helped guide the leadership team, Bill Allen became Boeing's first CEO without a formal engineering background.

Stage 3: Industry Leadership

First as a successful attorney and an early influential Boeing board member, and then as CEO, Allen changed Boeing from a war-time manufacturer to a large, successful multidivisional company. He proved to be the right leader for guiding Boeing into Stage 3 and to the forefront of the aerospace industry, where it reigned for more than a half of a century.

The preceding CEOs had focused more narrowly on creating and constructing the various functions of the corporation: Bill Boeing created the company and its powerful expert culture; Clairmont Egtvedt concentrated on aeronautical engineering and executing his "big Boeing" strategy; and P. G. Johnson built Boeing's mass production capability. In contrast, Bill Allen transformed himself into Boeing's first professional CEO business leader and led Boeing's growth to becoming the twenty-third billion-dollar revenue company in the United States in 1954.

With the board's approval, Allen made the decision to build the Dash-80 prototype, later renamed the Boeing 707 jetliner. For a second time, the company launched the industry game-changing product with the Dash-80's maiden flight in 1954 and the first commercial 707 delivery in 1960.

Peacetime prosperity in the U.S. economy and affordable intercontinental jet-age travel gave more and more of the U.S. population the opportunity to visit foreign countries. Understanding other cultures and values became a challenge for companies as well as for individual Americans during the Cold War, as U.S. corporations started working with outsourcing partners and selling American products in other countries. Under Bill Allen's CEO leadership, in 1968, Boeing rolled out its third industry game-changing product, the giant Boeing 747, and went on to dominate the commercial airplane market by building a family of jet aircraft for worldwide sales. Its revenue growth was organically fueled, and the company continued to grow into the next stage.

Stage 4: Globalization and Diversification

Large multiproduct, multibillion-dollar revenue corporations were becoming commonplace during the 1960s and 1970s. To cope with the complexity, these growing corporations typically decentralized operations by product or geography and assigned planning and management control to a relatively small centralized corporate headquarters. At the same time, the "big eight" professional accounting firms (e.g., PriceWaterhouse, Peat Marwick, and Arthur Anderson) and large management consulting firms (e.g., McKinsey and Boston Consulting Group) grew rapidly to assist corporations in establishing decentralized structures and systems. Boeing reorganized its ever-growing and increasingly difficult-to-manage commercial airplane unit by creating smaller units to manage each airplane product line: 707, 727, 737, and 747.[10] This further decentralization gave Boeing an organization structure that consisted of four levels: Level 1, corporate headquarters; Level 2, business units (Commercial Airplane and Aerospace); Level 3, product groups; and Level 4: functional departments.

Another important capability that long-lasting corporations learned and developed is managing through situational crises. The Boeing Corporation had managed through at least three near-death crises: breakup and restructuring forced by U.S. antitrust litigation,[11] building a mass production factory for complex airplanes, and transitioning from a war-time military supplier to a successful peace-time manufacturer of commercial airliners.

Bold and decisive actions are necessary to lead a corporation through crisis while preserving a strong company culture. At no other time is the CEO's leadership more challenged from both inside and outside the company. The CEO's every action is watched closely, and strategy, integrity, and fairness remain under the microscope.

This is also a time when a careful process of CEO succession is truly tested. Bill Allen's approach to identifying candidates to succeed him as CEO, and then choosing among them, required major CEO and board time, effort, and judgment.

Allen picked two strong senior management leaders from within the company as finalist candidates and then mentored both of them as they developed the abilities to be his successor. One was the legendary aeronautical engineer Thornton "T" Wilson. Wilson had distinguished himself by leading the design and manufacturing of the X-47 big Boeing military prototype, thereby pioneering much of the technology and innovation for the commercial version: the Dash-80, which eventually became the Boeing 707. Wilson was notorious for emphasizing the all-important Boeing culture of "manufacturing to perfection." He personally inspected the airfoil surfaces of B-47s and B-52s to make sure that the rivets were wet sanded to be perfectly flush to ensure minimum drag on the airplane skin surfaces.

Allen's second candidate was John Yeasting, one of Boeing's strongest CFOs. Yeasting was hired away from Boeing's auditing firm and distinguished himself by offering a balancing voice to the strong engineering culture advocated by Bill Allen: "if we build the best airplane, customers will buy it." The imbalance here was that the quest to build the best airplane engendered an environment where the design engineers tended to ignore cost implications.

At this juncture, Boeing had evolved to a point where either a subject matter expert (such as an accomplished aeronautical engineer) or a professional business manager (such as the CFO) could qualify to become CEO. Either would need to be especially careful to "know what they don't know" and compensate by building a senior management leadership team well rounded in the company's subject knowledge base as well as its business and competitive challenges. Simply stated, the successful CEO of the emerging large corporation had to balance two important countervailing factors: product excellence and profitability.

Allen chose T Wilson to be the next CEO but stayed on as board chairman to mentor and be available to Wilson for a few years before turning the board chairman job over to him as well. Wilson managed Boeing through the worldwide recessions of 1969–1970 and 1973–1975, the latter triggered by the quadrupling of oil prices in 1973, which resulted in a huge decline in airline orders for new commercial airplanes. He radically restructured the company to fit the new realities of marketplace demand, preempting private equity firms from buying a controlling interest and doing the same thing. Wilson downsized Boeing's headcount from 100,000 to 38,000. His aggressive and decisive action saved the company, but he never got over firing all of those people. Here, we learn another subtle aspect of managing the company's culture. If draconian decisions like massive layoffs ever come too easy, the CEO impugns his ability to lead the corporation. Especially during those inevitable stressful times, the CEO is ultimately responsible for maintaining the company culture and the trust of its multiple constituencies.

Wilson proved himself by getting Boeing through its severe financial crisis while maintaining the company's culture and, indeed, its very soul as employees understood it. Wilson also used and strengthened Bill Allen's comprehensive successor selection process. After an extensive, long-running search, in April 1986, Wilson and the board turned the CEO reins over to a formally trained business professional, Frank Shrontz—a trained lawyer and Harvard Business School MBA graduate from outside the company. Shrontz went on to lead Boeing through a decade of solid growth, retaining its industry-leading position and more than doubling its stock price.

Responding to the troublesome commercial airplane boom-and-bust selling cycle, Boeing experimented with diversification and globalization in Italy and Japan. Future CEO Phil Condit worked with Italian companies on the joint development and manufacture of a small, one-hundred-passenger commercial airplane. Boeing also worked with the Japanese on a joint commercial airplane design and manufacturing venture. Neither venture resulted in a jointly built airplane, but both engendered long-term outsourcing partnerships with companies in those countries, as well as closer relationships between Boeing and the respective governments.

Boeing's diversification initiatives extended to related as well as unrelated business ventures. In 1970, the company consolidated its thirteen internal computing organizations into a wholly owned subsidiary called Boeing

Computer Services. BCS served Boeing's internal operations and also sold computing services to outside customers, including the U.S. government. Unrelated or loosely related diversification ventures included hydrofoil boats for both military and private use, mass transit light train equipment and systems, and windmills for power generation. In all, Boeing entered into thirty-three diversification ventures and eventually exited all of them. The company learned to do many things, but its cost structure, workforce, and culture were designed for competitive advantage in the aerospace industry, not for a profitable conglomerate. By the late 1980s, the inefficient complex conglomerate organization structure was further challenged by emerging technologies and new, more nimble organizational forms.

Stage 5: Transformation

A long run of industry leadership can easily lead to complacency: "why change what we are doing if we are the industry leader?" Boeing's management was aware that Airbus continued to make inroads in the commercial airplane market, but shrugged it off with little sense of urgency. Nevertheless, Shrontz recognized the need to reposition the company to continue flourishing in the new competitive environment. Together with the board and the senior management team, he concluded that doing the same things that had made Boeing an industry leader in the twentieth century would not suffice. In 1996, he and the board chose Phil Condit as president and directed him to ensure that Boeing retains industry leadership into the twenty-first century.

The competitive environment was changing in ways that incremental initiatives seemed unable to address. More than half of the one hundred largest organizations in the world were corporations. The others were sovereign countries. The two largest corporations, ExxonMobil and Wal-Mart, were headquartered in the United States, but operated globally, as did Boeing. Like Boeing, these corporations were interlocked with strategic partners, international suppliers, and customers, and were influenced by multiple governmental bodies.

Corporations had changed in size, scope, and structure. Workers and their work were very different than in the past. The number of factory workers had declined in a manner reminiscent of the decline of farm workers in the twentieth century. Blue collar/white collar work categories blurred, and the majority of jobs increasingly came to be described as knowledge work. Most of the younger workers were digital natives who had grown up with nonstop access to ubiquitous information technology. Diversity in the workforce had changed from low to high; loyalty to the corporation had gone from high to low; and the rate of job changes had gone from nil or low to high.

Intangible cost factors exceeded the tangible cost factors for both products and services. The product/service concept had evolved to focus on "lifecycle costs." Decision making had evolved from a slow heartbeat paced on annual budgeting to a fast pulse paced on real-time information. Corporations were now global in their structures, workforces, and markets.

Highly controlled vertically integrated structures had morphed into horizontal virtual networks of global partners; tight ownership control had given way to coordination based on trust, information transparency, and shared objectives. Management orientation had shifted from production-driven efficiency to customer-driven effectiveness—with production-driven efficiency as an obvious prerequisite. Innovation had shifted from episodic and sporadic to continuous and strategic. In short, many of the most effective twentieth-century CEOs would not have survived the leadership demands placed on twenty-first-century CEOs.

In subsequent chapters, we will explore the consequences of these transitions of business transformation:

- from vertical integration to virtual integration
- from decentralized structures to networked global partnerships
- from in-house mass production to extensive outsourcing
- from co-located operations to geographic dispersion with an evolving concept of industry commons
- from national to global purview
- from product-driven to customer-driven orientation
- from annual/quarterly budgets to dynamic, real-time adjustments
- from "command-and-control" leadership to collaborative senior teams
- from spectator sport to participatory sport in managing IT

A most dramatic change was the importance and formalization of the process of leading the corporation with respect to vision, strategy, and execution.

Vision creates a concept of the longer state for a company. It is multiyear in timeframe, often extending to future decades, but not precise in the exact timeframe specified. Visions must maintain relevance to the realities of the world economy and the desired market position for the company. Good visions serve as inspirational and motivational backdrops for the workforce.

The vision is the short story of the being of the corporation; it's the précis. It has coherence and resonates in binding people together into a coherent, collaborative force to realize the inspirational goal.

Strategy broadly outlines how the vision will be pursued and provides direction on the key decisions involved. For example, IBM's strategic decision to offer integrated systems rather than breaking into separate product-oriented companies broadly outlined how IBM's vision would be pursued. Boeing's strategic decision to incorporate acquisitions to become a more balanced aerospace company outlined how Boeing's 2016 vision would be pursued.

In a fast-changing global economy with incessantly developing competitive threats, a company's strategy needs to be constantly monitored and adjusted to remain a "good strategy." A good strategy serves as a dynamic road map for guiding collective effort for the corporation toward its shared vision.

Execution involves the one-year plan (and often two- and three-year plans too) and the specific resource allocations required to achieve the plan. Detailed operational budgets specify the company resources devoted to achieve specific goals. Financial metrics are specified to determine the extent of achievement of goals and are often extended to nonfinancial metrics such as customer satisfaction in determining goal achievement.

IT real-time monitoring of goal achievement of one-year plans has enabled dynamic resource allocation, sharpening the efficiency and effectiveness of a company's execution processes. To some extent, real-time monitoring is organic and has obsolesced quarterly and annual budget variance analyses for monitoring goal achievement.

The financial news on August 10, 2012, underscored the twenty-first-century reality of corporations whose shared visions and strategies drive execution with tech-savvy collaborative workers and partners. That day, the thirty-five-year-old Apple Corporation's market value exceeded $600 billion, making it the highest valued company in the world, surpassing Exxon-Mobil Corporation. This new world was the world into which the Dreamliner project was born, as part of Boeing's new 2016 vision and strategy. Although unarticulated at the time, the new aircraft's overarching purpose was nothing short of a product-driven transformation of the entire company.

The mechanic who yelled out after the Dreamliner maiden flight, "It flew because we made it fly," wasn't quite right. He and his fellow mechanics were only part of the plot, or story; they were the craftsmen, or makers, who put the physical parts of the Dreamliner together. They were collaborators with other makers: engineers and managers. Creative aeronautical engineers designed the parts and conceived of the interrelations and interfaces among the parts that made up a flying airplane—an artifact made up of millions of physical parts all flying in perfect formation five miles high in the sky. Professional managers built the workspace and systems enabling the airplane to be created, whereby ideas were implemented establishing the interrelationships of the physical parts—ideas every bit as important as the millions of physical parts of the airplane.

The story and plot resulting in the Dreamliner included Boeing management, creative designers, craftsmen, pilots, and Boeing's partners and global outsourcers. So the Dreamliner flew because all of these people successfully collaborated on making it fly. While the mechanic who yelled out wasn't quite right, he was right about something else. He was right that Boeing had not yet resolved the conflict among its thousands of makers in transforming to a successful twenty-first-century corporation.

In chapter 2 we take a closer look at the ways in which this new world, and this new program, differed from Bill Boeing's and his successors' experiences in the many years before.

NOTES

1. Boeing's industry game-changing products included the Boeing 247 all-metal structural airliner, Boeing 707 jet airliner, and the Boeing 747 giant airliner.
2. See YouTube video of 787 rollout: www.youtube.com/watch?v=VZW_GnJ6YtQ, accessed by author on January 7, 2012.

3. Dominic Gates, "Boeing Unveils 787 Dreamliner in Worldwide Production," *Seattle Times*, July 7, 2007. Photograph by Mike Siegel *Seattle Times*. The 787 shown in the photo was Plane 1, and it was far from a complete airplane and would never fly commercially. The 787 that would be successfully certified by the FAA would be Plane 4 on August 26, 2011. The first 3 787's would be written off as R&D expense.
4. Compared to the 1967 Boeing 737, the Boeing 787 had expanded closer to 3 million parts due to the increased sophistication of commercial airplanes. In addition, the commercial airplane had now become an integral part of a broader global system of inflight commercial airplanes including flight control and maintenance systems.
5. This description is expanded in my article: Richard L. Nolan, "Ubiquitous IT: The Case of the Boeing 787 and Implications for Strategic IT Research," *Journal of Strategic Information Systems*, 21 (2012), 96–98.
6. Norris, G., and Wagner, M., *Boeing 787 Dreamliner* (Minneapolis: Zenith Press, 2009), p. 76. This well-illustrated book is accessible and comprehensive on background and development of the Dreamliner.
7. Although Boeing commercial airplane–designed wings had been a proprietary secret for years, the competitive advantage has been somewhat minimized by competition. Nevertheless, Boeing strived to protect their perceived competitive advantage by designing and building the fixed and leading moveable edges of the wings.
8. Active aerospace industry and Boeing blogs were alive, citing various senior-level positions going to McDonnell-Douglas executives including the Boeing COO and President (Harry Stonecipher), CFO (Michael Sears), and board positions (John McDonnell and Harry Stonecipher).
9. Clairmont L. Egtvedt, upon retirement from Boeing, continued to serve as board chairman until 1966.
10. The assignment of names for Boeing commercial airplanes started off with the third digit representing the sequential number of the airplane, and then, with the exception of the 707, and the second digit represented the next airplane in the 707 family to be manufactured. The 727 was the second in the 707 airplane family. Extensions of the family member were designated by three following digits. For example, the 727–100.
11. U.S. antitrust litigation became a rather frequent hazard for some of the most successful U.S. companies in the twentieth century, including Boeing, the Great Atlantic and Pacific Tea Company, IBM, and Microsoft.

BIBLIOGRAPHY

Gates, Dominic, "Boeing Unveils 787 Dreamliner in Worldwide Production," *Seattle Times*, July 7, 2007.
Kotha, Suresh, and Nolan, Richard, "Boeing 787: The Dreamliner," Harvard Business School Case #305–101. Revised June 21, 2005.
Mansfield, Harold, *Vision: A Saga of the Sky* (New York: Duell, Sloan and Pearce, 1956).
Nolan, Richard L., "Ubiquitous IT: The Case of the Boeing 787 and Implications for Strategic IT Research," *Journal of Strategic Information Systems*, 21 (2012), 96–98.
Norris, Guy, and Wagner, Mark, *Boeing 787 Dreamliner* (Minneapolis: Zenithy Press, 2009).
Serling, Robert J., *Legend and Legacy: The Story of Boeing and Its People* (New York: St. Martin's Press, 1992).

2 Then and Now

Bill Boeing got his first taste of flight on July 4th, 1915, on the shores of Lake Washington in Seattle, where barnstormer pilot Terah Maroney was offering airplane rides to the paying public. Maroney was touring the United States with his flimsy bi-wing, wooden and fabric airplane—not much more advanced than the Wright brothers' first airplane. As a lark, Boeing and his friend, Navy Lieutenant G. Conrad Westervelt, took their first airplane ride, and after several more, they were smitten. On the spot, they decided to build a better airplane. It was Bill Boeing's second major business venture, personally financed by the wealth he had amassed earlier in timber along with the taconite mining rights that he foresaw and secured in acquiring timberlands.

Boeing soon traveled to Los Angeles for flight training with Glenn Martin, a pioneering pilot there. Westervelt sought advice from academic and practical airplane experts. The two set up shop in a former Seattle shipyard in a red barn.[1] They contacted Herb Munter, the local Seattle exhibition flyer who was building his own primitive airplane, to join the team as test pilot. After taking measurements from Maroney's airplane, reviewing the Wright brothers' patents, and consulting Jerome Hunsaker, who had established a wind tunnel at MIT, the team began building their first airplane. A little less than a year later, they had designed and built the B&W (for Boeing and Westervelt) seaplane. On June 15, 1916, Boeing himself piloted the B&W on its maiden flight. It weighed 2,600 pounds and had a wingspan of 52 feet, a cruise speed of 67 mph, and a range of 320 miles.[2]

Bill Boeing was the epitome of the impatient, persistent, risk-taking, prescient visionary who acts on what few can see. His vision of airplanes became an obsession, and his twin mottoes—"Build to perfection" and "Let no airplane technology pass us by"—helped move the world of travel far beyond the fragile wood, baling wire, and fabric machines of the time.

The nascent U.S. road network was still very poor. Only in 1903, after sixty-three days from California to New York on the Oregon Trail, had the first men successfully driven an automobile across the continental United States.[3] Not until the Eisenhower presidency in the 1950s would there be a modern continental road system. During the first two decades of the twentieth century, trains took five to six days to cross the United States, averaging 25 to 35 miles per hour. Ninety-five percent of intercity travel was done by train, but it was an arduous undertaking for individual passengers forced to deal with multiple private railroad companies to get from one place to another. The new B&W seaplane flew at speeds much faster than any other mode of transportation. And little new infrastructure was required: the aircraft only needed a lake or a small body of water to take off and land.

NOW

Three quarters of a century later, in 2013, thousands of land-based airports buzzed with daily activity, connecting major cities with the remotest hinterlands all over the world. An estimated 12,000 out of a total of 16,000 in-service commercial airplanes were Boeing owned or leased and operated by some 900 different airlines. With 2013 revenues of more than $86 billion, the Boeing Company was viewed as one of the United States's most valuable national assets.

Boeing, ranked among the biggest, most successful corporations in the world, seemed poised to excel in the twenty-first century. Yet its future was far from guaranteed. Rivals such as Airbus, the giant European consortium; Embracer, the smaller but feisty Brazilian firm; and Quebec-based Bombardier were heating up the competition. New opportunities and obstacles were constantly appearing on the horizon, such as the Republic of China's aggressive pursuit of building its own global presence in aerospace and the commercial airplane industry. China and Japan were also threatening the air travel market with investments in high-speed trains that were approaching jet airplane speeds.

Chapter 1 described five stages of evolution common to the corporate giants that grew up in the twentieth century and survived to struggle for relevance in the twenty-first. For our purposes in this chapter, we distill three broader eras in the lives of these companies: Start-up (Stage 1), Life after the founder (Stages 2–4), and Transformation to the new economy (Stage 5).

Skillfully navigating the era of life after the founder more or less defines our most successful twentieth-century organizations. Nevertheless, it is by comparing the start-up phase with the essential post-2000 transformations (Stage 5) that we learn the most for guiding these venerable corporations into the new economic realities of the twenty-first century. Indeed, the task that faces today's executives as they transition to the new century is similar, in many ways, to that of the founders many decades ago.

A NEW STRATEGY FOR A TRANSFORMATIVE ERA

By the 1990s, Boeing's leaders were planning intensely for the challenges of the coming decades. Their predecessors had successfully grown and reshaped the company (and the industry) several times during its long history. Now it was time to begin the process again.

Phil Condit, recently appointed president and a member of the board, put together a high-level task force to create a strategy for the twenty-first century. The group began with one of the most fundamental strategic questions: what kind of company do we want to be?

It quickly became clear that there were many things Boeing wasn't good at. As for one, Condit put it, "Boeing was zero for 33"—that is, the company had a dismal track record for its periodic forays into nonaerospace businesses. The project team concluded that Boeing needed to "stick to its knitting," and that there remained a lot of opportunity in the aerospace sector.[4] This was not a surprising conclusion, as many corporations were moving away from the conglomerate structures popularized in the 1970s and 1980s.

The next question was: what was Boeing *really* good at? The project team explored core competencies but became stuck when the list included pretty much everything Boeing currently did. Condit questioned the team's logic, starting at the top of the list: wings.

Condit: "Why are wings a core competency of Boeing?"

Answer: "Boeing has always built the wings."

Condit: "Airbus builds wings, and today there are only 2 to 4 percentage points between the efficiency of a Boeing-built wing over an Airbus-built wing. When considered as an integral part of the airplane, a 2 to 4 percentage advantage in efficiency is miniscule. So today, why should we spend our scarce research and engineering resources building wings?"

Comment by project team member: "We originally built wings because we had to; there was no way to efficiently transport wings any distance to our final assembly line."

Condit: "Is designing and building wings a Boeing core competency?"

Answer: "Yes, because the wings are such an important system of a commercial airplane."

Condit: "So is the jet engine, and Boeing doesn't build jet engines for its airplanes. So is the landing gear, and Boeing doesn't build the landing gear. And so are the avionics, and Boeing is building less and less of the avionics. Based on my reading and thinking, our core competencies must be capabilities that we can do uniquely, and capabilities that our competitors would have a hard time copying."

Condit and his team decided that a company could nurture no more than two or three core competencies, or in the rare exception, four. Any more would diminish its ability to focus and allocate resources.[5] Accordingly, they identified three core competencies:[6]

- **Large systems integration.** The principles of large-systems integration ran deep in the Boeing culture. They were embedded in every new line of commercial airplanes that the company had developed. The team considered systems integration skills a major competitive advantage for the company.
- **Detailed customer knowledge.** Employees throughout the organization gained detailed knowledge of customers' needs through daily contact with the airlines as they operated and serviced Boeing airplanes around the world.
- **Lean manufacturing and reliability.** Boeing's lean manufacturing capabilities, first developed in the run-up to WWII, incorporated constant innovation as part of a flow, as typified by the continuously moving 737 final assembly line.[7] Moreover, Boeing excelled in building reliability during the test flights and certification, as well as in its Airplane-on-the-Ground (AOG) program.

So the team articulated a new statement about core competencies as follows: that Boeing must become a knowledge- and resource-sharing company that excels in the design, manufacture, and support of commercial aircraft, defense, and space systems, and that it should continue its global leadership in core competencies such as the integration of large, complex[8] systems, with detailed customer knowledge and focus on operating lean and efficient systems.[9]

While Boeing had operations in all three subcomponents—commercial aircraft, defense, and space systems—80 percent of the company's revenue came from commercial airplanes in 1996. The Condit task force concluded that being a healthy aerospace company in the twenty-first century would require better balance among the three key markets: space, defense, and commercial airplanes.

Space is where major research breakthroughs occur. Defense is characterized by one-off or short-run manufacturing of military airplanes and other defense systems. Generally, leading aerospace research such as advances in composites is incorporated into military airplanes before commercial airplanes. Once proven in both design and manufacturing, these leading innovations find their way into commercial airplanes, where mass production produces major revenues and profits. Also, commercial airplanes have long operating lives, which provides major revenue opportunities for airplane system services.

To remake Boeing as a balanced aerospace company, the strategy team chose to depart from its tradition of organic growth and seek acquisitions in both space and defense businesses that could offset its commercial airplane business imbalance faster than would be possible through organic growth alone. Setting aside the discussion about acquisitions for the moment, the team went on to address organizational structure. The new strategy and the acquisition program resulted in restructuring Boeing into three business units, each with its own CEO: commercial, defense, and space. And the approach to manufacturing would change dramatically.

At the time, Boeing built airplanes on a final assembly line, in a process known as "stick building" manufacturing, or what today's experts would call a pulse assembly line. Fabricated commercial airplane parts were brought to a manufacturing plant, and the airplane was constructed on an assembly line. Over the years, outside suppliers were assembling more and more of the parts of the commercial airplane into completed systems. Condit's team concluded that twentieth-century "stick building" would not sustain the company into the twenty-first century. Instead, they intended to convert Boeing factories from pulse assembly lines to continuously moving assembly lines, eventually "snapping" together complete major component systems as if they were assembling Lego model parts.

The trend was toward using a network of global outsourcers to manufacture major subsystems such as engines, wings, and avionics. One reason for this trend was the increasingly sophisticated specialization of systems such as computer-based avionics. Another was the continued insistence by countries (such as China) with large commercial airplane markets that more of the design and manufacturing tasks be done in their countries by their workers.

Condit and his team envisioned building a different kind of Boeing entity: a virtually integrated organization with strategic partners spanning the globe. The new format would use advanced IT to support more customer-driven product design and manufacturing. The company would change from an aerospace manufacturer with building commercial jet airliners as its major business to a large aerospace systems integrator with a balanced mix of space, defense, and commercial airplane businesses.

GETTING FROM WHERE WE ARE TO WHERE WE WANT TO BE

In addition to core competencies, business strategists need to consider multiple forces within the company and in the environment. In established companies like Boeing, they need to think about fitting the existing corporate structure, culture, and vision to evolving market structure, competitors, suppliers, and customers, while incorporating emerging technologies and the threats/opportunities they represent. Those responsible for execution must make sure that all of the millions of moving parts come together and fit together.

Trail-blazing entrepreneurs, from Elisha Otis to Bill Boeing, to Bill Gates, to Steve Jobs and Sheryl Sandberg, often find themselves inventing or reshaping these elements as they go along. For example, there were no books on how to build a successful company or create a new industry to help Bill Boeing; he had to figure it out for himself. He had to deal with the typical obstacles such as hiring and firing, cash flow, and creating a market. But what was it that enabled the company to flourish beyond its founder to achieve and retain industry leadership? The first part of the answer is found in what Bill Boeing—the original company creator—actually *did* during his eighteen years at the airplane company. He communicated a compelling vision for the future of flight. He created an organization—a business. He developed core capabilities to supplement his own: aeronautical science and engineering, operations and manufacturing, test piloting, and sales and marketing. He created a culture of engineering design excellence, technology friendliness, and manufacturing perfection. He kept the company afloat during hard times, never wavering from his vision. He created the Puget Sound high-tech infrastructure and environment necessary to succeed, expanding access to talent and expertise. And he made the right product and created the market for the United Aircraft and Transport Corporation, later the Boeing Company. Although not all parts of the company that Bill Boeing created would remain together, each was built to last.

Condit and his colleagues had to *reinvent* Boeing to enact the 2016 strategy. This meant recognizing and respecting the legacy of their predecessors while addressing the challenges of the future. Essentially they needed to balance bold creativity with careful stewardship to keep the company healthy while transforming it. The strategy team got off to an aggressive start. They launched programs to achieve the following:

- grow revenue through strategic aerospace company acquisitions
- restructure the Boeing organization to a more balanced aerospace company
- revolutionize airplane assembly from a pulse line to a continuously moving line
- transform the company with a game-changing new commercial airplane program

MAINTAINING COMMERCIAL AIRPLANE INDUSTRY LEADERSHIP

Condit's creator skills flourished in meeting the Airbus challenge by bringing out a new commercial airplane product. Together with Boeing's Commercial Airplane CEO, Alan Mulally (a career Boeing engineer, who worked his way up into executive management), Condit had begun a joint study with Airbus called the VLA (Very Large Airplane) Project. As the project progressed, Condit and Mulally had doubts about the commercial feasibility of a VLA.

For one thing, the new super-jumbo airplane envisioned was based on the assumption that it would work in concert with the hub-and-spoke airport system. In other words, the large airport hubs like New York, London, and Tokyo would continue to dominate, and smaller airplanes would continue to fly into such hubs to consolidate large numbers of people for long-haul flights on super-jumbo airplanes.

Condit and his team concluded that the congested hub-and-spoke system was reaching its limits. Accordingly, the Condit team searched for alternatives. They created a potentially game-changing challenge to the hub-and-spoke system: point to point. The idea was to fly people long distances directly to where they wanted to go, when they wanted to go. The plan was to build a fuel efficient, medium-sized airplane that could fly to smaller, less congested airports around the world. The more the Condit team studied the alternative, the more convinced they became that a point-to-point airplane was a better approach than the super-jumbo airplane. They set out to design a new breed of plane that would outpace the Airbus VLA, and code-named the new craft the Sonic Cruiser, even as Airbus remained fixated on attacking Boeing's dominance in jumbo jets.

Boeing and Airbus subsequently dissolved their joint exploration of a super-jumbo airplane and chose to go their own ways. Airbus, however, still wanted to build a very large airplane, one that would help them neutralize Boeing's jumbo jet monopoly. Some industry observers wondered whether Boeing had used a *"million dollar head-fake"*[10] to trap Airbus into building the A380, but it's difficult to say.[11]

Condit recalled Boeing's assessment of Airbus: "We were in a position where Airbus was challenging us in assuming the industry leadership position. They were going to build another long-range A310 replacement. If they had done that, instead of the A380, they might have wrestled the industry leadership from us. We would have been in the game, but clearly been in second place."[12]

"We concluded Airbus could do three things: First, they could build a 220-passenger, long-range jet. And if they did this, we thought that we have big problems, because this could harm the 777. Second, they could build a 747 type of airplane. With the data we had, we reasoned that would have killed the 747. Third, they could build a huge airplane like the A380. . . . Clearly, we knew they were going to do something because their business model was not to lay off engineers. . . . Once their engineers came off a new airplane development project, they would have to go right into the next new airplane project."[13]

Condit suggested that Airbus's intense focus on neutralizing Boeing's perceived advantage in the very large airplane market was misguided. Airbus, he noted, assumed that Boeing was using profits generated from 747s to subsidize its smaller family of airplanes: "If you make the assumption that

Boeing and Airbus are equally efficient at building all their airplanes by the 'pound of airplane,' you come to the conclusion that most of Boeing profitability comes from the 747 jet. But the reality is that the 747 is much harder to build than, say, the 737 airplane, and, so it is not a huge contributor to the company's profitability. . . . Fact No. 1, Airbus truly believed that Boeing was making a whole bunch of money on the 747, and using it to subsidize programs like the 737. Fact No. 2 was that Airbus could more easily sell to their various government sponsors. Big airplanes were associated with prestige, and thus were an easier political sell. And, Fact No. 3, [was their idea] that we [Airbus] will never be credible until we produce a large airplane that supplants Boeing's 747. . . . My view, not shared by all of the Boeing management team, was that a large airplane was not economical, and if Airbus did it, it would put them in strategic jeopardy."[14]

It is unlikely that Boeing entrapped Airbus into building a super-jumbo jet. Airbus, it appears, was fixated on a super-jumbo for many reasons. It is also clear that once Airbus committed to such an airplane, Boeing was happy to cede the market. Moreover, it didn't want to do anything to jeopardize Airbus from pursuing this path. In fact, Harry Stonecipher, then Boeing COO, has been quoted as telling his Boeing colleagues: "We must not do anything to drive them away from that airplane."[15]

Mike Bair, Boeing's strategic planner, was even more blunt: "The A380, we concluded several times over, didn't make sense. It is never going to generate a return, which was our conclusion when we looked at whether we should do a big plane. Part of this is, when you do something like this airplane, there is sort of a rule of thumb that is called the square-cube law. The law states that as the airplane size squares, everything else cubes, so it runs away from you really fast. It ran away from us [when we did the 747 plane]. . . . So we were happy that Airbus decided that this market was a good place to spend their money and efforts. It has consumed them and will continue to consume them for a long time. They [Airbus] for all practical purposes have conceded the bottom end of the twin market to us."[16]

Around 2000, Boeing focused on a new program to design and build an industry game-changing commercial aircraft: a medium-sized, long-haul commercial airplane with breakthrough efficiency employing carbon composites for structural and skin components.[17]

GAME-CHANGING INDUSTRY STRATEGIES

The Boeing Corporation has maintained its commercial airplane industry leadership through bold initiatives that involved executing industry game-changing strategies: the Boeing 247, the Boeing 707, the Boeing 747, and now its Boeing 787 initiative. None of these were airplanes that could be described as incremental strategies; they were all bold strategies that anticipated and changed the industry structure. Figure 2.1 shows Boeing

Figure 2.1 First Boeing Commercial Passenger Airplane and Modern Dreamliner Flying Together

Model 40, the first Boeing airplane to carry passengers, flying in formation with the Boeing 787–8.

The Boeing Model 40 had capacity of two to four passengers, and flew at 128 miles per hour with a range of 650 miles—(its first flight took place on July 20, 1925). The 787 family of airliners have passenger capacities from 242–323, range of 7,850–8,300 nautical miles, and cruising speed of Mach 0.85—i.e., 85 percent of the speed of sound).

As we review the twenty-first-century competitive environment, successful corporate strategies tend to be more bold and directed at industry structural change than the incremental, less bold strategies characterizing the twentieth century. The Apple Corporation led by Steve Jobs embraced a corporate strategy to "change the world." When Apple hired seasoned CEO John Sculley in what was later referred to in disdain as bringing in adult supervision, the company changed to a more incremental strategy of "milking" existing products. Steve Jobs left Apple in disgust at the change in strategy. Afterward, Apple's industry performance increased to record revenues, but then degenerated to near bankruptcy, leading to the return of Steve Jobs. Jobs then went on to continue his bold strategy of creating game-changing industry products and led Apple back from the abyss.

Jeff Bezos, founder and CEO of Amazon, came out of nowhere to create a strategy and execute it to change the retail book industry, on the road to changing the overall retail industry itself. He built a virtual bookstore—the biggest bookstore in the world—and then virtualized the physical book and followed up by virtualizing the entire shopping experience. The CEO of Otis Elevator, George David, created and executed an industry game-changing strategy to transform Otis Elevator from an elevator manufacture to an elevator service company.

There are many differences between THEN and NOW, and, most importantly, several extremely important differences. First, NOW requires corporations to embrace, more than ever, bold rather than incremental strategies. Competitors can respond to incremental strategies much more rapidly than to bold strategies.

Second, effective and efficient execution of industry strategies has become more difficult partially due to the increased size and global complexity inherent in the increasing globalization of competition. Further, the shift from vertical integration to virtual integration has reduced direct control in coordinating outsourced activities and requires more difficult collaborative coordination of corporate activities. And corporations are encountering a steep learning curve in mastering new capabilities required to effectively coordinate activities in the extended organizational context of virtually structured corporations.

Third, during the last half of the twentieth century, corporations scaled to billion-dollar enterprises largely through the assimilation of professional managers and mastery of formal management principles and techniques. Innovation was episodic and biased towards incrementalism. Now, bold strategies involve sustained innovation, and more balance in the corporation between managers, or stewards, and those who create, or innovate.

NOTES

1. Many years later, the red barn was moved to the Boeing Museum of Flight, where it can be seen today.
2. Boeing History, "Heritage of Innovation," www.boeing.com/history/, accessed by author, July 7, 2011.
3. Driving an automobile from coast to coast in 1903 was a difficult and daring achievement. H. Nelson Jackson, a physician and businessman from Burlington, Vermont, captured the nation's attention when he and Sewall K. Crocker, a mechanic, drove from California to New York through mud, washouts, and breakdowns. They finished their trip in sixty-three days. See *Horatio's Drive: America's First Road Trip* by Dayton Duncan and Ken Burns (Alfred A. Knopf, 2003).
4. Proctor, Paul C., "Boeing Ascendant," *Frontiers*, 1, no. 1 (May 2002).
5. Nolan/Condit video interview, March 1, 2010.
6. *Ibid.* In an updated Boeing background dated July 20, 2012, the 2016 strategy was reprinted as "Boeing's vision."
7. Condit toured Japanese factories to study Japanese management and lean manufacturing. He was so involved with the Japanese processes that he received a doctorate in engineering from Science University of Tokyo in 1997.
8. Subsequently, the term "complex" was eliminated. While the systems were complex, Condit said, there was no inherent objective to make them complex. In fact, the emphasis was more on simplification.

9. Nolan/Condit video interview, March 1, 2010.
10. One of the participants in my HBS ExecEd classes during the summer of 2006 blurted out "head fake" as we discussed the joint Boeing-Airbus study on the potential of a super-jumbo aircraft program. The participant had a background in aerospace. A head fake is a sports term used to describe a player using his head to fool an opponent.
11. John Newhouse, in his book *Boeing Versus Airbus*, says no: "What we know is that Airbus felt strongly pushed to complete a family portrait of its airplanes with a very big one and thereby prove that the company's improbable blend of corporate cultures and divergent methods could match Boeing's most conspicuous accomplishment, the 747." Newhouse, John, *Boeing Versus Airbus* (Alfred A. Knopf), p. 150.
12. Nolan/Condit video interview, April 10, 2008.
13. *Ibid.*
14. *Ibid.*
15. Newhouse, *Boeing Versus Airbus*, 150.
16. Nolan/Mike Bair interview, July 24, 2008.
17. On October 12, 2002, Phil Condit gave the keynote speech at MIT Sloan School celebrating Sloan's 50th Anniversary. In this twenty-minute address and twelve minutes of questions and answers, Condit describes his CEO leadership of Boeing and Boeing's transformation strategy into the twenty-first century. It was during this period that I discussed these ideas with Condit and then decided to accept the Boeing Philip M. Condit chaired professorship at the University of Washington in January 2003 to engage with Boeing and conduct the research for this book. See the video of the keynote: http://video.mit.edu/watch/philip-condit-keynote-speech-9872/, accessed by author on April 14, 2014.

BIBLIOGRAPHY

Boeing History, "Heritage of Innovation," www.boeing.com/history/, accessed by author, July 7, 2011.

Condit, Philip M., keynote speech at MIT Sloan School celebrating Sloan's 50tth Anniversary, October 12, 2002, http://video.mit.edu/watch/philip-condit-keynote-speech-9872/, accessed by author on April 14, 2014.

Duncan, Dayton, and Burns, Ken, *Horatio's Drive: America's First Road Trip* (New York: Alfred A. Knopf, 2003).

Newhouse, John, *Boeing Versus Airbus* (New York: Alfred A. Knopf, a division of Random House, 2007).

Proctor, Paul C., "Boeing Ascendant," *Frontiers*, 1, no. 1 (May 2002). www.boeing.com/news/frontiers/archive/2002/may/cover.html, accessed by author on September 22, 2014.

3 Creators and Stewards

The entrepreneurs of the twentieth century were almost by definition creators, not professional managers with the skills to scale their enterprises to billion-dollar revenue corporations. The United States spawned unique industries and professions such as venture capitalists, accountants, and business consultants, who funded and infused professional management into start-ups, enabling many to scale into multibillion-dollar corporations.

During Stage 2 and 3 in the growth of the corporation as described in chapter 1, almost as a manner of course, the founding entrepreneur was considered to get in the way of growth, and often left, either by being "kicked upstairs" (demoted from CEO to a lesser position) or out-and-out fired to make way for the stewards or professional managers to take over unfettered. The emerging corporate professional management team, or stewards, mastered the techniques that became known as scientific management, which enabled scaling production of the product or service created by the entrepreneur, often to grow to billion-dollar revenue enterprises.

Eventually, this pattern ran its course, and often the first real threat to the continued growth of many of the first-mover corporations came from imitators or fast followers. Then the corporation faced the challenge of bringing out a new or an improved product line or service to sustain its growth. Many corporations never succeeded with such follow-on products. But of course, many did succeed. Those twentieth-century corporations that did succeed—such as Boeing, IBM, Otis Elevators, and others—learned to manage a seemingly awkward partnership with the entrepreneurial contributors in their midst, who were often called scientists, engineers, or simply creators.[1]

Both creators and stewards were necessary to maintain the corporation's relevance and sustainability over time. Occasionally, one role or the other took the fore, as, for example, when Egtvedt created the "big Boeings" strategy and championed the B-247 and the derived B-17 as a company-advancing follow-on product to Bill Boeing's earlier airplane designs. Later, Bill Allen promoted creator Thornton "T" Wilson, and Wilson brought to fruition the designs that led from the Dash-80 to the game-changing B-707. The legendary aeronautical engineer, Joe Sutter, was considered the driving creative force behind the next game changer, the B-747.[2]

Some of Boeing's leaders supplemented their creative activities with learned stewardship skills, and some stayed more solidly in the stewardship camp. Philip Johnson revolutionized Boeing's manufacturing capacity with mass production to enhance profitability. Bill Allen, the first non-engineer to take the reins, built a solid organization to lead the industry by creating a family of jet airliners.

T Wilson, an engineer and aerospace design expert, was forced to downsize employee headcount by some 60 percent to save the company, yet he never lost sight of the need to preserve the elements of its creative company culture. During the hard times, Wilson allowed one of his talented aeronautical engineers to persist in redesigning the 727 in one of Boeing's most celebrated "skunks works"—the Boeing 727–200.[3]

Frank Shrontz, the first formally trained business professional to run the company, successfully grew and strengthened Boeing to maintain leadership among its rivals of the 1980s and early 1990s. Arguably, each one of these CEO leaders maintained the right balance between creativity and stewardship to serve the needs of his time.[4]

One of the biggest challenges in maintaining this balance can be described as the contrast between the mindsets of creators and stewards in corporations.[5] The dichotomy is conceptual, but the characteristics have resonated with both innovators and managers in corporations as they have struggled to maintain an essential balance between the two types.

Creators embrace grand visions and focus on the innovations necessary to realize the visions. Their mindset extends beyond daily work concerns as they commit their intellectual talents and intrinsic motivation to realizing the corporate vision. In contrast, stewards are generally more committed to the "law of diminishing returns" to support their interest in maximizing the financial performance of the corporation—that is, stewards don't want to invest one dollar past the point where the immediate return drops off. The crux of the conflict is allocating resources of the corporation between longer, more uncertain innovations to create new products and services versus more certain, shorter-term products and services. Whereas stewards look for "good enough," innovators tend to see "good enough as not good enough."

Maintaining a good balance requires a deep understanding of how the perspectives and behaviors of stewards and creators differ. Figure 3.1 draws contrasts among characteristics that often differ between stewards and creators.

Most managers who oversee innovation processes are inclined toward the steward's point of view. As corporations have grown during Stages 2 and 3, more and more pressure has been levied on measurable short-term metrics such as earnings per share and return on investments—metrics that most creators remain oblivious to as they pursue longer-term goals. Antagonism often results, leading to breakdowns in communications between the two.

The fallout from imbalances is legend in corporate history: IBM failed to recognize the importance of microcomputer technologies while milking

	Stewards	Creators
Governing motivation	Allocates corporate resource responsibly	Realize the grand vision at all cost
Motivation on point of diminishing returns	Good enough is good enough; going beyond diminishing returns is bad	Don't know where diminishing return is, and don't care; good enough is not good enough
Motivation to compromise	Required as part of many practical business solutions	Not to be considered when pursuing an important vision
Always in mind	What's the business model?	What's the big picture, and is it important to mankind?
Value	Value capture	Value creation

Figure 3.1 Differences between Stewards and Creators in Corporations

Source: From Robert D. Austin and Richard L. Nolan, "Bridging the Gap Between Stewards and Creators," *MIT Sloan Management Review* (Winter 2007), Vol. 48 No. 2, pp. 29–36.

their mainframe product too long; Xerox failed to see the potential of their research in creating personal computer systems, and allowed and partially enabled Apple to commercialize the Macintosh personal computer.

The Apple board of directors drove Steve Jobs away and sacrificed the long-term future of Apple for short-term profitability. Apple milked their existing product line while failing to innovate new products, and the corporation plunged into near bankruptcy. After firing the CEO who replaced Steve Jobs, the then CEO brought Jobs back to create a new line of products including the iPod, iPhone, and iPad. Jobs's creative leadership propelled Apple to a market value of $600 billion on April 10, 2012, making it the most valuable public company in the world at that time.

Eastman Kodak invested in emerging digital photography technologies, but it failed to invest enough to change the company culture so that it could successfully commercialize and sustain a competitive digital photography product line. On January 19, 2012, after more than one hundred years of operation, Eastman Kodak filed for Chapter 11 bankruptcy and become only a shadow of its glory days.

THE CLASH OF CULTURES AT BOEING

During the last half of the twentieth century, modern corporations continued to get bigger; multibillion-dollar corporations became commonplace. Accounting was refined as an ever-present management tool. Business unit profit and loss statements and capital investment models moved to center stage in managing the big, multidivisional corporations.

The General Electric (GE) conglomerate was a leader in accounting-based management, contributing to the popular adage: "A good manager can manage anything"—that is, management expertise could prevail over subject expertise in managing large corporations.

But nearing the twenty-first century, that assertion began to lose its wide acceptability. Financial engineering in corporations seemed to have run its course with respect to increasing shareholder value. Corporate strategists started to refocus on core competencies and the specific cultural capabilities of each organization.

A widespread realization began to emerge that no one person or CEO could embody all the capabilities at the depth required to lead the ever-growing complexities of multibillion-dollar revenue corporations. Incumbent on the CEOs of big corporations was to know what they didn't know and build a trusted, well-functioning executive leadership team that incorporated the blend of broad and in-depth skills of creators and stewards, while maintaining a delicate balance between the influence of the team that possessed the respective skills.

Unfortunately, the Condit team's earliest implementation of organizational restructuring initiatives at Boeing proved disappointing, particularly as the company tried to absorb its ambitious acquisitions. First came Rockwell Aerospace Company, in August 1996. Later that same year, Condit led the acquisition of longtime competitor McDonnell-Douglas—a $17-billion revenue company with a troubled commercial airplane business but a healthy defense business. These transformational decisions were made at stealth speed and hailed by the business press. *Fortune* magazine called the McDonnell-Douglas acquisition the "sale of the century."[6]

But the unprecedentedly large McDonnell-Douglas acquisition shocked Boeing like nothing before. It altered the make-up of the board and introduced the challenge of amalgamating two very strong company cultures. The McDonnell-Douglas culture, strongly embodied in John McDonnell, Harry Stonecipher, Jim McNerney, and Michael Sears, all of whom joined Boeing's executive management team and/or the board, leaned heavily toward accounting-oriented stewardship. Following the acquisition, John McDonnell became the Boeing board's largest single shareholder, and Michael Sears was named corporate CFO. Harry Stonecipher (named President and Corporate Chief Operating Officer, and member of the board) and James McNerney (who by that point was CEO of 3M and a new board member at Boeing) were former GE executives, steeped in the widely respected management-by-numbers culture that was seen and refined as the brainchild of Jack Welch, one of America's most successful twentieth-century business leaders.

During this time, Airbus continued to close the gap between it and Boeing in manufacturing "very good" commercial airplanes, and it had been aggressively pricing its commercial airplanes to undercut Boeing's prices. Bill Allen's strategy of "build the best airplane, and the airlines will buy it" had run its course. Boeing factories had gradually lost their cost advantage. Airbus began outselling Boeing.

Condit had seen this coming and had encouraged his senior management to study Japanese lean manufacturing practice to increase the efficiencies of Boeing factories. But these factory programs had not reached fruition by the time Airbus was manufacturing competitive commercial airplanes selling for lower prices than Boeing.

Not yet able to match Airbus' lower cost profile, Condit and his senior management team responded by dropping the price of their airplanes to remain competitive. Boeing's order book rebounded. But in October 1997, the increased production was too much for the traditional factories, causing control and supply chain problems and the shutdown of two major Boeing assembly lines. The shutdown cost Boeing $2.6 billion and caused one factory manager to be replaced. For 1997, Boeing reported its first loss in fifty years: $178 million. Wall Street analysts turned from praising Condit to criticizing him brutally. Boeing's share priced toppled from $106 to $49.

Dejected and frustrated with the pace of improving factory efficiency, Condit fired eighty senior executives. This, too, represented a culture shock, unheard of since the late 1960s when T Wilson had to reduce the Boeing workforce from more than 100,000 to 38,000. While Boeing had rather routinely made relatively large layoffs and rehired factory workers and engineers with the ups and downs of airplane orders, senior management had been largely buffered from such cuts.

The typical Boeing way to deal with senior management performance problems had been to put the troubled performer into what was informally referred to as the "penalty box." There the manager would have only token responsibility but was given the opportunity to work his or her way back to significant responsibility.[7] Those who succeeded often expressed their appreciation of the lessons learned. But Condit's mass firings shattered any semblance of illusions of loyalty in the management ranks.

Condit seemed to have become enthralled with the GE management style, leaning in the direction that McDonnell, Stonecipher, Sears, and McNerney began taking Boeing—that is, stewardship with greater emphasis on financial metrics. Economic value focus tended to pull Boeing away from its engineering culture creator roots.

In this context, the Boeing Corporation encountered the classic steward/creator conflict with the "go/no-go" decision to approve the 787 program. The steward in this case, Boeing's new CEO, Harry Stonecipher, who replaced Phil Condit, tipped the balance to the steward's side. Stonecipher and the board seemingly found comfort in a global network of partners willing to co-invest in developing the airplane. The result, intended to significantly reduce the financial risk of a new commercial airplane, came with an extraordinary increase in risk for Boeing, arising from the unprecedented global outsourcing of engineering design and manufacturing of major 787 components such as the wings and fuselage.

During the second half of the twentieth century, the pendulum balance between subject matter expertise (generally associated with innovation) and business expertise (generally associated with strengthening profitability, or the bottom line) remained delicate. The debate about creators and stewards has remained an important one for boards of directors in selecting their twenty-first-century CEO leaders and discharging their duties of effective corporate performance oversight.

NEW THINKING FOR A NEW CENTURY

The twenty-first century requires new thinking about stewards and creators and the corporation. While the twentieth century saw the scaling of corporations through mass production and globalization, creating new products and services was subjugated to a process that could be described as punctuated innovation—mostly incremental innovation. Typically, it wasn't until a product or service reached the latter stages of its lifecycle (or beyond) that corporations heavily focused on the creation of new products and/or services. The prevailing strategies of becoming number 1 or number 2 in revenue and/or market share or selling the business unit tended to motivate corporations to extend their leading products beyond their natural product lifecycle.[8] As companies focused on extending product lifecycles rather than inventing new products, the creators were directed to develop patent portfolios for existing core products, so that armies of corporate lawyers could fend off competitive imitators. Too often, the unintended result was an extended window for competitors to create new products, further eroding the profits of the incumbents as their internal creators languished in the land of stewardship.

But this approach wasn't working so well in the times of corporate globalization and real-time information flows enabled by the Internet and IT. Instead of extended product lifecycles and a process of elongated punctuated innovation, fast-cycle prototyping and sustained innovation have become the new reality. The awkward steward/creator partnership has given way to new thinking about the relationship. The relationship that had been imbued in conflict has had to change to one of cooperation and collaboration to meet the corporate challenges of the twenty-first century characterized by shorter product lifecycles and a sustained innovation process that quickly incorporates innovations into the product line.

FROM AWKWARD PARTNERSHIPS TO MULTIDISCIPLINARY COLLABORATION

Something else was changing too in the twenty-first century competitive environment. The process of innovation was becoming more collaborative among groups of entrepreneurs and corporations. And the overall process of innovation seemed to be spanning longer time periods, resulting in more complex products enabled by the diverse collaboration opportunities. Indeed, the Boeing 787 new airplane product was a reflection of the nature of the new process.

It was the early signs of this new process in the corporate environment and the apparent need for sustained innovation rather than punctuated innovation that motivated my Harvard Business School colleagues and me to launch a research study to learn more about the collaboration enabling the Internet to come about. The Internet was not the result of a sole corporation—although both AT&T and IBM tried, each in their own way. The Internet came about through sustained innovation by a group of collaborators from different institutions (both universities and businesses spanning the globe) over a period of more than thirty years. A compelling vision provided coherence and a collaborative emergent strategy. Execution led to all the interrelated components being built and coming together to create the Internet as we know it today.

Our research efforts expanded beyond our original collaboration at the Harvard Business School. I went on to the University of Washington to launch the Seattle Innovation Symposia—a joint undertaking with the Foster School of Business, the Computer Science Department, and the Information School—and to carry out case research on Boeing's innovative Dreamliner program.

My colleagues in this research, Rob Austin and Shannon O'Donnell, left the Harvard Business School to join the Copenhagen Business School in order to conduct multidisciplinary research on innovation. The Copenhagen Business School had developed a creative program combining the arts and management disciplines in studying innovation. Two dissertations by our research assistants,[9] four books,[10] including this one, and a number of academic journal articles and cases have been produced from our team's collaborative efforts.

Mass production has now become an accepted and important component of economic activity, and innovation in the corporation must also become similarly understood and carried out as a sustained process. A prerequisite to balancing the influence of stewards and creators is understanding the influence of the existing corporate culture, and how to change it to maintain relevance. In chapter 4, we address the importance of awareness about what the corporate culture is, and the challenges of changing it to what it must become to accommodate twenty-first-century corporate performance.

NOTES

1. Austin, Robert D., and Nolan, Richard L., "Bridging the Gap Between Stewards and Creators," *MIT Sloan Management Review*, 48 no. 2 (Winter 2007), 29–36.

2. Sutter, Joe, 747: *Creating the World's First Jumbo Jet and Other Adventures from a Life in Aviation* (Harper Row, 1997). Also, Phil Condit was a member of the 747 design team and contributed several patents during the development of the airliner.
3. In a hidden, low-profile, informal operation referred to famously as a "skunks works," Jack Steiner and his team persisted in bring out the 727–200 derivative, which was originally thought to be an obsolete airplane in light of the new wide-body competition: Douglas's DC-10 and Lockheed's 1011. After the Boeing Advanced 727–200 was introduced in 1970, more than half of all the 727s sold were Advanced 727–200s. Wilson publically acknowledged Steiner's skunk works: "Steiner, I don't know whether you designed the 727 or not, but I do know that you helped pay off our billion-dollar debt."
4. The story of Boeing leaders' individual and collective efforts has been told many times and is recounted vividly at Seattle's Boeing Museum of Flight. The Boeing museum website list public and private sources on Boeing history: www.museumofflight.org.
5. My colleague Rob Austin and I conducted research on the steward/creator conflict at the Harvard Business School and published the results of the research and our conclusions on managing the conflict in our article: Austin, Robert D., and Nolan, Richard L., "Bridging the Gap Between Stewards and Creators, *MIT Sloan Management Review*, 48, no. 2 (Winter 2007), 26–31.
6. Whitford, David, "Sale of the Century," *Fortune*, February 17, 1996.
7. One senior factory manager who had been put into the penalty box during the shutdown of a commercial airplane assembly line routinely came to my Boeing AIMS classes and spoke about the process. He had worked his way out and emphasized the Boeing culture of providing senior executives a second chance. While in the penalty box, the manager said his emails went from hundreds down to very few, with the Boeing house organ as a highlight.
8. This approach is often attributed to GE's "portfolio of businesses" strategy under CEO Jack Welch.
9. "Integration of Up and Downstream Activities: An Evaluation of the Pharmaceutical Industry," Erin Sullivan, Doctoral Dissertation, 2008, Trinity College, Dublin, and "Making Ensemble Possible in Distributed Groups: How Special Teams Organize for Collaborative Creativity in Conditions of Spatial Variability and Distance," Shannon O'Donnell, Doctoral Dissertation, 2013, Copenhagen Business School.
10. See *Adventures of an IT Leader* (2009), and *Harder Than I Thought* (2013) by Austin, Nolan, and O'Donnell, published by Harvard Business Press, and *Artful Making* (2003) by R. Austin and L. Devin, published by Financial Times.

BIBLIOGRAPHY

Austin, Robert D., and Nolan, Richard L, "Bridging the Gap between Stewards and Creators, *MIT Sloan Management Review*, 48, no. 2 (Winter 2007), 26–31.
Austin, Robert D., and Devin, Lee, *Artful Making: What Managers Need to Know About How Artists Work* (New Jersey: Financial Times Prentice Hall, 2003).
Austin, Robert D., Nolan, Richard L., and O'Donnell, Shannon, *Adventures of an IT Leader* (Boston: Harvard Business Press, 2009).
Austin, Robert D., Nolan, Richard L, and O'Donnell, Shannon, *Harder Than I Thought* (Boston: Harvard Business Press, 2013).
O'Donnell, Shannon, "Making Ensemble Possible in Distributed Groups: How Special Teams Organize for Collaborative Creativity in Conditions of Spatial

Variability and Distance," Doctoral Dissertation, Copenhagen Business School, 2013.

Sullivan, Erin, "Integration of Up and Downstream Activities: An Evaluation of the Pharmaceutical Industry," Erin Sullivan, Doctoral Dissertation, Trinity College, Dublin, 2008.

Sutter, Joe, *747: Creating the World's First Jumbo Jet and Other Adventures from a Life in Aviation* (New York: Harper Row, 1997).

Whitford, David, "Sale of the Century," *Fortune*, February 17, 1996.

4 Culture Is Everything

After eighty-one years of organic growth, Boeing's company culture had become among the strongest cultures of any corporation. It was one of Boeing's most important assets as reflected by many company practices and traditions. Boeing workers and their families often came together at Boeing Field to cheer lift-off of maiden flights of new Boeing airplanes. Mutual respect among managers, engineers, and mechanics was often manifested on the factory floor through humor and the easy "give and take" in a language understood only by insiders.

This cooperation could be observed every day at the 737 moving assembly line as a diverse group of engineers, managers, and machinists called the Moonshine Group roved around the line, observed, and engaged line workers on ideas and innovations to implement continuous improvements in the efficiency of the line.[1]

As a newly hired Boeing systems engineer and later as manager in the 737 branch, I began learning the Boeing company culture through stories about Bill Boeing, as well as other embellished Boeing legends, whenever they seemed relevant to the storyteller. In each of the stories, the consequences for violating an aspect of the company's culture generally included a hushed warning of serious repercussions such as being summarily fired. The stories often concluded with the storyteller's personal experiences about friends who suffered the consequences.

I also learned a lot from the advice of my manager who had been promoted up the line from factory management positions to Director. He encouraged me to spend time walking around the 737 factory floor, watching people work, and asking questions about why they do particular things the way they do.

Boeing's company culture was continuously strengthened by a tradition of promotion from within. It was also buffered from outside influences by the relative isolation of Puget Sound in the United States. Puget Sound was in the far Northwest (more than 3,000 miles west from New York and Washington, D.C.) and more than 1,100 miles north of Los Angeles and 800 miles north of San Francisco). Few people left the Pacific Northwest, and those that came tended to stay.

Maintaining, strengthening, and changing (when necessary) a company culture is one of the most important and challenging fiduciary responsibilities of a sitting CEO and the executive team. IBM CEO Lou Gerstner, speaking in 1994 to a Harvard Business School MBA class about the IBM transformation, made the point about the importance of company culture in no uncertain terms. Speaking softly and slowly, but in a strong voice for emphasis, he said, "Corporate culture is not just important, culture is everything."[2]

A company culture is mostly an intangible code largely learned by experience and reinforced by stories on "how we do things around here." It's partly explicit but remains mostly implicit. Gerstner went on to say that it took him to age fifty-seven to understand the importance of company culture and the difficult process of changing it. This is not atypical among today's CEO's in that for the last half of the twentieth century, corporate cultures were relatively stable and focused on production and sales processes. It's only into the second decade of the twenty-first century that corporations almost across the board are not only more aware of their corporate cultures but are also aware of the importance of managing cultural changes required for success in the twenty-first century.

Commenting on the HBS IBM case study that my colleagues and I had developed, Gerstner reflected that while studying for his MBA at HBS, he had a class including the subject of company culture: HBO. He quipped that it wasn't the television HBO that the students were familiar with. It was called "Human Behavior in Organizations." He joked, "Everyone hated it; it was touchy-feely stuff." Yet he continued, "It was probably one of the most important classes that I should have paid attention to." It was then that Gerstner made his personal comment that "culture wasn't just important, culture is everything."

This got my attention. I had recently been hearing similar comments from others. On the subject of Boeing's acquisition of McDonnell-Douglas, retired CEO Phil Condit said, "If I could have done one thing differently, I would have spent more time on company culture integration."[3]

The lesson on culture that Lou Gerstner shared with the HBS class was an important one during those emerging times of business transformation. Further, for many, it was a lesson that they had not been prepared to easily receive. And it is even harder to carry out because it entails figuring out what the corporate culture is, and how to change it for success in the fast-changing twenty-first-century global economy.

Echoing Gerstner's view, Condit reflected on the difficult nuances of learning about and changing a corporate culture. It struck him that the roots of Boeing's culture that Bill Boeing had established have sustained the company in subtle and not so subtle ways into the twenty-first century.

Condit mused about Bill Boeing as a lumberman who was incredibility intuitive about the potential of commercial air travel. More important was how he acted on his intuition and created the culture that enabled Boeing not only to emerge as a successful company but also to sustain that success over the years.

Condit then turned to another twentieth-century aspect of corporations: the importance and influence of the military model as the dominant organizational structure for building the gigantic twentieth-century mass production corporations like Boeing. He described the resultant culture of Boeing as similar to other successful twentieth-century corporations: as a mixture of the founder's legacy and accidental evolution. However, the dominant structure of the model had a number of inherent side effects such as workable, but cumbersome, hierarchical structures for communicating upward and downward and an intolerance for deviant behavior, which often resulted in factory cultures of "kick ass and take names" when any noncompliant behavior in the factory led to confusion in executing directions from the top.

Condit went on to say that in 1975 as chief engineer for the Boeing 757 program, he began to realize the importance of leaders able to more fully understand their corporation's culture, including the implicit impact of culture on decision making, motivation, and work. Later he led the team that launched the Boeing 777 airplane program and pioneered management concepts that integrated design/build teams of customers, suppliers, and employees to design and produce the 777. The 777 "Working Together" team received the prestigious aeronautical Collier Award for the extraordinary team collaboration that ultimately resulted in the Boeing 777.

Here Condit commented, that corporate leaders must (1) understand their corporate cultures and ensure that the culture is what it should be, and (2) tackle the exceedingly complex challenge of changing the institutionalized corporate culture to what is required to succeed in constantly changing environments. Changing a culture requires more than words and rhetoric; it involves what "you do." He went on to further describe corporate culture lessons from his work on the boards of Hewlett-Packard and Nordstrom.

"They watch your feet," Condit said, describing the program Nordstrom used to reinforce customer service culture. Every new hire—including aspiring Nordstrom family members—begins work in the shoe department putting shoes on customers' feet. This Puget Sound success story has propelled Nordstrom to industry leadership and has sustained its success through the leadership of three generations of the Nordstrom family CEOs.

Only three months on the job as General Motors CEO, Mary Barra found herself thrust into one of the biggest product safety crises in automotive industry history, requiring the recall of 7 million GM cars over a faulty ignition switch/cylinder. The flaw could cause certain GM cars to malfunction, cutting off the engine in traffic, and thereby disabling the power steering, power brakes, and air bags. The malfunctioning switch was linked to thirteen deaths and many serious crash injuries.

Documents submitted by GM to a congressional subcommittee showed that the total cost was an overbearing consideration when GM declined over a decade ago to implement fixes to the malfunctioning switch.[4] GM's investigation into the extent of the malfunction led to a recall of more than 20 million GM cars and trucks.

At a press conference following Barra's April 1, 2014, hearing before Congress, she said that it "angers me that we had a situation that took more than a decade to correct." Barra promised cultural changes at GM that would prevent such a lapse from happening again. "I think we in the past had more of a cost culture," she said, adding that it (the GM culture) is moving toward a more customer-focused culture.[5]

As I reflected on my own HBS teaching and the HBS MBA program in the 1970s, it became more obvious to me that the institutionalized bias among corporations then was highly slanted toward the costs; the intangibles such as culture were given relatively short shrift. The tangibles were more naturally associated with the numbers—especially the accounting numbers. Often heard in businesses and MBA classrooms was the adage: "If you can't measure it, you can't manage it."

Management theory then was often divided into formal systems like accounting, production, and sales and informal systems like human behavior and culture. Formal systems were easier to define and teach; informal systems were more amorphous and more challenging to teach; students with limited practical experience in business had difficulty grappling with discussions and learning about informal systems.[6]

Now more than ever, the culture change management challenge can be seen all around us. The Eastman Kodak Corporation led in consumer photography for almost a century. Then as chemical processing of film became increasingly challenged by advantages of digital photography, Kodak faced a corporate cultural management challenge to respond to the emerging disruptive technology. In meeting the challenge, it wasn't that Kodak did not recognize the importance of digital photography. In fact, Kodak's creative scientists built the leading digital photography patent portfolio, and today Kodak still holds many of the most important digital photography patents.

What resulted in Kodak's bankruptcy and disappearance from the industry that it led for so many decades was that the corporate leadership team either did not understand how fast better technologies were progressing, and/or it could not successfully manage the cultural change required by their workforce to change the way that Kodak worked.

Similarly to Kodak, IBM experienced a near miss in almost succumbing to the same mistake. But in contrast, the corporate leadership team led by outsider Lou Gerstner at IBM brought to bear a different perspective and was able to successfully manage the IBM corporate culture change, which changed the way that IBM was structured and worked—enabling IBM to remain viable into the twenty-first century.

Microsoft is another transformation with similarities to both Kodak and IBM that is playing out after CEO successor to founder Bill Gates, Steve Ballmer, retired and a new insider CEO was elected: Sarya Nadella. In a July 10, 2014, memo to Microsoft employees, "Starting FY15—Bold

Ambition & Our Core," Nadella says that "nothing is off the table" when it comes to reshaping the company culture to focus on users' productivity.[7] Then in a follow-up interview reported in the *Seattle Times*, Nadella stated, "Any strategy gets eaten for lunch if you don't have culture that backs it up."[8]

Major Acquisitions: Shock and Challenge to Healthy Corporate Cultures

Few events shock a corporate culture more than a major acquisition of another corporation, which presents the challenge of integrating different corporate cultures.

In 1997, shortly after Condit's promotion to CEO, with the stroke of a pen, Boeing acquired the McDonnell-Douglas Corporation. Instantly, Boeing's previous revenue from organic growth of $37 billion skyrocketed with an additional $17 billion to $54 billion.

Acquiring McDonnell-Douglas was like a fling in which Boeing woke up the next morning to find that it had married a partner that it really didn't know. A fawning press including well-respected *Fortune* magazine acclaimed the marriage. There were few naysayers to remind the marriage celebrators about the dismal record of corporations carrying off successful acquisitions—most disappoint and frequently become outright failures.

A classic National Bureau of Economic Research working paper, "Wealth Destruction on a Massive Scale?" by Sara B. Moeller, Frederik P. Schlingemann, and Rene M. Stulz found that from 1998 through 2001 the acquiring corporation's share price dropped 12 cents for every dollar spent for the acquisition.[9] And the record remains even more dismal if corporations face transformations requiring integration of diverse corporate cultures.

Both the McDonnell and Douglas corporations likely began by evolving cultures similar to Boeing's in embodying product technology and manufacturing excellence. But then, the Douglas Corporation became financially stretched with its DC-9 airplane program and invited merger/acquisition bids in 1966. Douglas Aircraft and McDonnell Aircraft merged in 1967.

The DC-10 was the first commercial airplane built by the merged companies. The program was begun in 1968, and first deliveries were made in 1971. On July 10, 1989, United Airlines Flight 232, a DC-10, en route from Denver to Chicago lost an engine, which severed the hydraulic lines required to fly the airplane. Using the remaining two engines for thrust to control the airplane, the DC-10 pilots crashed landed at Sioux City airport in Nebraska. Of the 285 passengers and 11 crew members on board, 110 passengers and one crew member were killed in the crash.

Investigations found that McDonnell-Douglas DC-10 had three back-up hydraulic systems, but in UA Flight 232, a punctured section resulted in a total loss of hydraulic fluid. Further sales of the DC-10 were stemmed by this widely viewed crash played around the world on TV news stations. The FAA grounded the entire fleet of DC-10s. In 1989, McDonnell-Douglas cancelled the DC-10 program.[10]

Subsequently, hydraulic fuses were incorporated in McDonnell-Douglas MD-11s to isolate a punctured section and prevent a total loss of hydraulic fluid, but the damage was done. McDonnell-Douglas continued to struggle with its commercial airplane sales.

McDonnell-Douglas continued to use financial engineering to leverage a dwindling set of assets, while casting off poor performing assets—including many rounds of layoffs. By the time of the Boeing acquisition in 1997, the financial engineering culture had come to dominate McDonnell-Douglas.

THE CRITICAL CHALLENGES OF CHANGING TWENTIETH-CENTURY COMPANY CULTURES

As we said earlier about Boeing's transformation, two of the three essential components were put in place: vision and a good strategy. Phil Condit's successor as CEO in 2003 (Harry Stonecipher) confirmed Boeing's 2016 strategy, and Jim McNerney, who took over as CEO from Stonecipher in 2005, confirmed it again in 2005.

The third component, execution, continued to falter. The execution of the spearhead 787 product-driven transformation slowly stumbled along with an occasional bright spot such as the successful maiden flight, and the subsequent 787 certification that allowed the game-changing airplane to be finally integrated into airline fleets. But even then a series of 787 commercial airline flights had made emergency landings because of in-flight problems with the airplane's electrical systems. Further delivery delays followed.

Upon the landing of the 787 maiden flight, when the mechanic yelled out that "it flew because we made it fly," he spoke of a relatively small group of 787 engineers and mechanics who changed the way they worked to rescue the troubled plane. But the Boeing company culture was far from changed and integrated. Boeing's last three CEOs had faltered in integrating a common Boeing culture, which contributed to missteps in executing the 787 program execution in the first place.

In a highly controversial decision, Condit moved Boeing's headquarters to Chicago in 2001. This geographical move continued to fragment Boeing's company culture by geographically separating and isolating the senior Boeing leaders from the all-important strategy of using the Dreamliner to spearhead the company's product-driven transformation to a twenty-first-century corporation. The corporate executive team not only inhibited the means to know what was going on with the 787 program but also impeded their earlier goal of capitalizing experiences from the program in understanding transformation and extending its appropriate processes to other Boeing Corporation programs.

Condit defended the move by claiming that it brought him and his senior team closer to the home of a major customer (United Airlines) and afforded easy access to other airline customers who used O'Hare Airport as a major international hub. Condit further claimed that the chief advantage was to give equal attention to all three lines of business defined in the 2016 strategy.[11]

At this juncture, it is important to note that Boeing had another tool to deal with geographical separation that was not fully exploited—namely, IT-enabled video communications. Boeing had and has some of the most advanced IT systems in the world, as evidenced by their leading-edge PLM/CAD/CAM systems for communicating in real-time complex 3-D engineering drawings, as well as their leading-edge use of virtual reality enabling engineers and executives to virtually "walk through" and experience an airplane not yet manufactured. As Boeing tended to become more IT enabled and virtually integrated with global strategic partners, there was no reason—other than the challenge of changing the way people worked and communicated—that the Boeing organization could not have leveraged IT-enabled communication to overcome some limitations of geographically dispersed organization units.

Alan Mulally, a career Boeing engineer who had been key steward/creator in the 777 program (and a favorite to succeed Condit as corporate CEO), was named CEO of the Boeing Commercial Airplane unit. With the move of corporate headquarters to Chicago, Mulally was more geographically isolated from corporate than ever before. Condit too had to sort out his own new leadership environment and cope with the cultural implications of the relocation.

These organizational moves weighed heavily on the company and its concerted ability to focus on creating the Dreamliner. The corporate-level stewards now in Chicago were focused on managing a diversified aerospace conglomerate with a bias toward financial engineering. The McDonnell-Douglas corporate culture continued pretty much as before the merger in the defense businesses. The Boeing corporate culture prevailed in the Puget Sound Commercial Airplane businesses but with a subtle shift emanating from Chicago that emphasized conglomerate-like financial engineering.

Then, the extended decentralization structure of Boeing's business units began to show cracks. Condit, as CEO and ultimately responsible for corporate missteps, became embroiled in a scandal over improper military procurement procedures.[12] The scandal resulted in Condit resigning as CEO. In the background lingered the critical tasks of recognizing and managing the profound differences between the twentieth-century environment and that of the new millennium.

CONTINUED INFUSION OF "GE-TYPE MANAGEMENT" AND CORPORATE CULTURE INTO BOEING

In filling the CEO leadership vacated by Condit, the board of directors called Harry Stonecipher out of retirement and elected him as CEO to succeed Condit. Stonecipher had a career very different than any other Boeing CEO.

In 1987 he became Vice President and General Manager of GE's jet aircraft business unit and was immersed in the GE management philosophy, which highly emphasized disciplined financial management metrics and industry leadership: "Be number 1 or 2 in the industry, or sell the business unit."[13] In 1994, Stonecipher became CEO of the troubled McDonnell-Douglas Corporation, whose stock was valued at $18 per share. By the time that the corporation was sold to Boeing in 1997, the stock was selling for $70 a share.

Stonecipher brought his GE/McDonnell-Douglas style of management to Boeing as COO/President and member of the board. Condit seemed to become a willing follower of financial management and economic value added (EVA) management. In addition, another GE executive alumnus joined the Boeing board in 2001: James McNerney, 3M CEO, and previously GE executive and contender to succeed Jack Welch as GE's CEO.

The most pressing decision Harry Stonecipher faced as newly elected CEO in 2003 was the new Dreamliner airplane program. The decision to go ahead with the Dreamliner would clearly signal Boeing's recommitment to the commercial airplane business[14] and all of the financial risks inherent in a new commercial airplane program. The issues involved amplified the differences between the institutionalized corporate cultures of Alan Mulally, CEO of Boeing's Commercial Airplane business, and Harry Stonecipher. Alan Mulally had spent his whole career to date at Boeing. He was fully immersed in Boeing's culture of designing leading-edge technology airplanes and building leading-edge technology airplanes and manufacturing to perfection, while striking a workable balance between creators and stewards.

Harry Stonecipher was steeped in the cultures of financial engineering with an eye on increasing shareholder value—with a preference heavily leaning toward stewards over creators. Stonecipher was alarmed by Boeing's new airplane investment risk and the increased expense exposure it entailed. The issues fueled heated discussion between Mulally and Stonecipher, resulting in a continuously strained relationship between the two.

The crux of the decision on go/no-go for the Dreamliner program came down to the extent of strategic outsourcing. The proposal that came to the board of directors was to build a revolutionary technological commercial airplane mainly using composites for major structural and airplane skin components (i.e., fuselage, wings, and empennage) and engage in global strategic outsourcing of major Tier 1 components in a manner that could be assembled into a finished airplane in three days' time. Strategic partners would be provided with "design to performance" specifications, which was a major departure from Boeing's historical process of providing outsourcers the more detailed engineering drawings. This new process would off-load significant investment burden and risk of the new airplane to Tier 1 outsourcers.

Board debate centered on the potential loss of control for Boeing, as the company would manage increased technology change along with massive strategic outsourcing of design and manufacturing. The combined challenges were seen as a build-up of more change and management challenges than Boeing had ever taken on and a magnitude that went against Boeing's tribal knowledge about taking on acceptable levels of change. An alternative was to cope with the magnitude of change by first building the 787 using mostly Boeing's traditional factories in order to master the process of manufacturing the new airplane. Afterward, the company could tackle the changes required for more extensively off-loading of manufacturing challenges to strategic partners.

Much of the strength of the alternative argument resided in Boeing's collective experience assimilated in its implicit corporate culture, which obviously was not and could not be fully expressed explicitly to the board members coming from diverse backgrounds and different company culture, two of whom were the majority board stockholders: John McDonnell and Harry Stonecipher.

New airplane programs at Boeing required a unanimous vote of the board, and unprecedented levels of outsourcing to off-load Boeing investment risk prevailed as the price for the board of directors' unanimous approval. The influence of mixed corporate cultures muddied the waters in respect to the board fully understanding the implications of this decision as debated by Alan Mulally and Harry Stonecipher. The board approved the Dreamliner program on April 26, 2004, deciding to carry through with unprecedented global outsourcing along with the process changes in working with Tier 1 outsourcers from "build to print" drawings to "build to performance."

UNPRECEDENTED CHURNING AT THE TOP

There are few disruptions of a corporate culture that have such a major impact on the performance of a corporation as unstable CEO leadership. With the forced resignation of Condit, Boeing's CEO leadership was further destabilized, which exacerbated an already confused corporate culture and weakened the 787 program leadership, as well as the overall Boeing corporate leadership.

Stonecipher's tenure as CEO was short lived. The board was surprised when it was discovered that Stonecipher was carrying on an affair with a Boeing female employee. On March 7, 2005, a mere fifteen months after he became CEO, the board ousted Stonecipher as CEO and board member for poor judgment in respect to Boeing's code of ethical conduct.

On that same day, the shaken board appointed Boeing CFO James A. Bell as interim CEO and launched a search for a new Boeing CEO. The search quickly boiled down to board member and 3M CEO, Jim McNerney, and Alan Mulally. On July 1, 2005, the board elected James McNerney as Boeing CEO and Chairman. Lew Platt resigned his position as nonexecutive board chairman, and became Lead Director of the board.

Jim McNerney would be only the second outsider to serve as Boeing CEO.[15] McNerney grew up in the Midwest. He studied liberal arts at Yale and went on to the Harvard Business School for his MBA degree. He had a storybook background leading up to his career at GE.

After HBS, he gained diverse business experience as a brand manager for Procter & Gamble and strategic consulting experience at McKinsey & Company, including working in Germany. Seven years out of HBS, he joined the management team at the General Electric Corporation. McNerney was mentored by GE CEO Jack Welch and rapidly rose in the GE executive ranks. His long GE career included holding positions as President of GE Information Services, EVP of GE Capital, President and CEO of GE Electrical Distribution and Control, President of GE Asia-Pacific, President and CEO of GE Lighting, and President and CEO of GE Aircraft Engines.

After not being selected as Jack Welch's CEO successor in 2001, McNerney left GE to become CEO and Chairman of the 3M Company. McNerney took the GE management philosophy and culture to his new CEO position at 3M and over the next five years, he increased 3M's revenue from $16.7 billion to $21 billion.

The 3M Corporation was considered one of the most innovative companies in the world. William McKnight, who became general manager in 1914 and retired as CEO and Chairman in 1966, established 3M's deep innovative culture. Under McKnight's CEO leadership, sustained innovation resulted in one third of 3M's revenue coming from products that did not exist four years earlier.

McKnight made the research laboratory a central part of 3M rather than having the research labs geographically separated. He followed a looser management philosophy compared to his contemporaries, allowing 3M scientists to follow their ideas. His philosophy was that if the scientist is essentially right himself, his mistakes are not as serious as the mistakes an overbearing or dictatorial management team can make. McKnight translated his philosophy into a 3M principle that became part of 3M's strong culture: "If you put fences around people, you get sheep." Much of the success of 3M can be attributed to the innovations that resulted from the delicate balance between 3M stewards and creators that McKnight instigated and maintained.

McNerney became CEO of 3M during a time when 3M's financial performance had dropped off and the economy was in the midst of recession. He aggressively shocked the creator-oriented 3M culture with his steward-oriented GE culture, including programs to slash costs, rationalize purchasing, improve and centralize business processes, and undertake 6-Sigma quality initiatives. He instituted an in-house executive education program similar to GE's Crotonville program, whereby "leaders taught leaders" in the way that GE did with its own company-owned and -run education campus.[16]

McNerney led the 3M Corporation to improved financial performance, but not without controversy. His critics bemoaned that under McNerney's CEO leadership, 3M side-tracked its historical culture of sustained innovations for short-term profits.

McNerney left 3M to become Boeing's CEO in 2005, so it is hard to say whether his 3M tenure and GE approach transformed 3M or whether the situation was more like the Apple Corporation experience with John Sculley. Sculley's leadership at Apple propped up Apple's financial performance in the short run but left the company with no pipeline of innovative products to sustain the corporation in the longer run. When this became obvious, Apple's board of directors fired Sculley.

McNerney had joined the Boeing board in 2001 while Condit presided as CEO and struggled to implement the 2016 strategy. Two years later, he participated as a board member in the forced resignation of Condit, and the selection of Stonecipher as the new CEO. Stonecipher and McNerney shared background in the GE approach to management including decentralization, executive accountability, and focus on the financial numbers—skewing the balance toward stewards versus creators at the newly restructured Boeing corporation.

After becoming Boeing CEO, McNerney spoke to a reporter on how he sized up Boeing and his approach for leading the company forward. McNerney said Boeing's strategy and financials are in good shape, ". . . so my focus will be on the fundamentals. . . . It'll be on customers, it will be on deepening my knowledge of the operations, it will be learning the specifics of what's going on, the strengths and weaknesses of some of our people . . . to take some deep dives into the technology here. [It] is awesome and its deployment is a critical decision. . . . [My approach] will be less on big structural or financial or strategic fixes, more becoming part of the team."[17]

On that same day, while being interviewed from his new Boeing Chicago Headquarters office, McNerney told a *Seattle Post Intelligencer* reporter that ". . . the first order of business is to get the 787 done."[18] McNerney continued with a litany of priorities, including: ". . . winning back the confidence of Congress in the company as a defense contractor."[19]

Slowly but steadily, McNerney set out to do what he said he was going to do. Alan Mulally, CEO of the Commercial Airplane business unit, continued to clash with McNerney and soon left Boeing. McNerney replaced Mulally with Scott Carson, a nontechnical, long-term, respected Boeing executive. While Carson was of the Boeing historical culture with a slight tilt of the balance toward creators over stewards, as reflected by Boeing's persistent engineering orientation, Carson himself was a trained and experienced steward. So again Boeing loaded up on the steward side and diluted the creator side, further edging toward stewardship orientation in the changing Boeing corporate culture.

Two years later at 6:32 p.m. on April 25, 2007, the first Dreamlifter landed on schedule at Boeing Paine field and disgorged the major 787 components to be "snapped" together into Plane 1. This would be the last time that any milestone of the original 787 plan would be achieved as scheduled.[20]

In the meantime, a charade of "everything is okay" persisted while panicked Boeing Everett workers scrambled to cobble together the set of 787 components that they received to build a facsimile of the first 787. Plane 1 was physically rolled out on 7/8/2007 for the public to see on the *Today Show*, but it had custom-fabricated fake parts, some fabricated from the same plastic composite materials used for racecar moldings to look like a flyable 787.[21]

But even at this late date the official maiden flight of the 787 remained scheduled for August 2007 and first deliveries for May 2008 in time for China Airlines to fly spectators on new 787s to the 2008 Beijing World Olympics. Neither would happen.

Cynicism ran rampant through the Boeing Commercial Airplane business units, with the SPEEA[22] union referring to the extensive 787 outsourcing as the failed Hollywood model. They contended that Boeing assumed that they could also bring independent contractors (such as actors, camera operators, publicists, and the like) on a project basis for many movies (or commercial airplanes), avoiding the expenses of having all such staffers constantly on the payroll. Referring to Boeing's extensive outsourcing for the 787 as the Hollywood model, the SPEEA legislative director, Stan Sorscher, understated, "Staffers and project teams are not easily interchangeable in manufacturing products as complex as jets."[23]

The McNerney leadership team could not continue the charade that all was well with the Boeing 787 program. There was no way to finesse the manufacture of a high-tech new airplane program that has to perform flawlessly in flying passengers thousands of miles close to the speed of sound five miles up in the sky. The McNerney leadership team had to face the music of their execution problems and formally tell their customers and shareholders about their problems that would delay deliveries from the contractual schedules, triggering unprecedented penalty costs.

McNerney had participated in the Boeing board debate on approval of going ahead with the Dreamliner program while Stonecipher was CEO in 2004. Shortly thereafter in 2005, McNerney became CEO and then Chairman too. All of the subsequent delivery delays occurred during McNerney's tenure as CEO and Chairman of the board. While not all of the 787 execution problems were a result of McNerney's decision making, the overall execution of the program was under the purview of his leadership. And effective CEO leadership of the 787 program during the execution of the design and manufacture of the airplane faltered.

The first delivery delay was formally announced on October 10, 2007, and deliveries were pushed out six months from May 2008 to November or December 2008. In announcing that first delay on October 10, 2007, McNerney cited difficulties with final assembly of the first 787 and part shortages in the supply chain. Four weeks earlier, McNerney had voiced confidence in meeting the May 2008 delivery date to Japan's All Nippon Airways. McNerney's credibility with 787 airline customer executives was impugned, and he lost further credibility with Boeing Commercial Airplane workers.

The McNerney team reacted by firing some of the 787 program executives—characteristic of the GE philosophy of holding executives accountable and quickly replacing them upon performance problems. Mike Bair was removed as Vice President and General Manager of the 787 program and succeeded by Pat Shanahan.[24] Both had grown up in Boeing and were promoted from within. Pat Shanahan built a strong team including Steve Westby, Scott Strode (a talented Defense Systems executive), Ross Bogue (a self-made Boeing executive) and Jeffrey Stone.

A severe part shortage problem was tracked to airplane fasteners. The GE culture admitted no excuses for such shortcomings. But the problem here was that there was no information transparency throughout the tiered global supply chain. The shortage of fasteners seemed to be triggered by the exceptionally high sales bookings for 787s. A number of Tier 1, Tier 2, and Tier 3 suppliers began hoarding fasteners, which, in turn, resulted in shortages throughout the global 787 supply chain. Scott Strode was the fall guy and transferred to a more limited role in troubleshooting 787 manufacturing problems that outsourcer strategic partner Vought was experiencing. Later Strode was transferred out of the 787 team and back into the Integrated Defense Systems business unit. Russ Bogue took his turn in the 787 caldrons. He was replaced and sucked up the consequences of the difficult job that he was given.

Problems with the outsourced flight-control software also contributed to the delay. The outsourcer's uncertainty about effectively resolving complex software problems was seen as particularly troublesome. Again, the prevailing GE-style management culture, in this case of not disclosing problems until solved, was inappropriate for dealing with the severity of the problems in manufacturing a commercial airplane.

The second delivery delay, announced by the McNerney leadership team on January 16, 2008, stretched the schedule by an additional three months. This delay too was due to major problems with global outsourcers. Pat Shanahan, now the 787 program executive, told industry analysts, "We underestimated how long it would take to complete someone else's work."[25]

At this point, the extent of delivery delays triggered penalty costs for Boeing, at the time estimated to amount to around $1 billion. Boeing had booked more than eight hundred advanced 787 orders with a combined value of more than $100 billion.

The third delay was announced on April 9, 2008. This delay was not months, but a year—to the third quarter of 2009. Under the revised delivery schedule, Boeing would now deliver twenty-five planes to 787 customers by the end of 2008—less than a quarter of what the company had promised to deliver that year. Steve Westby, who had performed a thankless task in taking over an impossible global manufacturing job for the 787, managed the "roll out" of Plane 1. He survived the first two formally announced 787 delivery delays but was replaced after the third announced delay. Westby took early retirement, leaving Boeing in May 2008.

The maiden flight for the 787 was now delayed to the fourth quarter of 2009. Prior to the maiden flight, static testing revealed structural integrity problems with the wing box, requiring added weight to correct. The added weight impacted the range estimates for the airplane, which was troublesome to a number of 787 airline customers who planned to put their new 787s into service on long-haul routes. Brake testing revealed heat problems impacting the overall braking systems that had to be resolved. Overly stressed 787 electrical systems that had replaced hydraulic systems caused fires to break out in early 787 test airplanes.

Scott Carson, understandably, back-pedaled in providing revised delivery schedules. Now airlines questioned Boeing's 787 overall program airplane delivery forecasts. Boeing had never before experienced new airplane delivery delays to this degree.

On August 31, 2009, the McNerney leadership team announced the sudden departure of Scott Carson as President and CEO of Boeing Commercial Airplane. McNerney now had been at the helm as CEO for four years. Carson had been a career employee with a solid reputation as an effective Boeing executive. His firing drew criticism from Boeing industry watchers of McNerney's leadership of the 787 program. McNerney had been CEO for two years while 787 program problems were being experienced but before the first 787 delays were announced. And the delays kept coming, along with the executive firings. During McNerney's last three years as CEO, he had been paid close to $60 million, while Boeing shares underperformed compared to the DJIA (Dow Jones Industrial Average Index).

The Carson firing triggered questions about why the board chose to fire Carson rather than McNerney, and some questioners noted that five new members were added to the board during McNerney's reign as CEO. The implication was that the board might not be holding McNerney to the high standards he was demanding of other executives.

Nevertheless, Boeing worked out these problems to the extent that the 787 maiden flight took place on December 15, 2009. It was not the first 787 that was rolled out for the *Today Show*[26] but the fourth 787 that successfully made the maiden flight.

The fact that the 787 successfully made its maiden flight tells us a lot about the traditional Boeing corporate culture and its depth. Designing, building, and flying a twenty-first-century high-tech commercial airplane is no small feat. To accomplish this feat in the context of a difficult acquisition, significant cultural influences by the acquired company's senior executive team and shifts in the make-up of the board of directors were monumental interferences. Yet the traditional Boeing commercial airplane corporate culture prevailed in coping with the interferences and collaboratively designed and built Boeing's fourth industry game-changing commercial airplane. The lesson here is that strong, effective corporate cultures are important corporate assets; they are hard to create and critical to corporate performance during turbulent times. Further, once created, the strong corporate cultures are resilient—especially during stressful times.

It also is cause for general reflection on the importance of global corporations as big and influential as national governments, being critical assets of our global economy. Accordingly, national government leaders should pay closer attention, and corporate leaders who find themselves in the privileged position of participating in the leadership of influential global corporations should reflect on the importance of their responsibilities, as should these corporations' boards of directors.

GOING FORWARD

The successful 787 maiden flight was of overwhelming importance in bolstering the flagging confidence in Boeing's ability to build and deliver the new 787 plane during its difficult assimilation of McDonnell-Douglas, and all the baggage that went with it—both internally and in outside relationships with airlines and partners. But the 787 manufacturing problems were far from over. Late delivery penalty costs had increased to a staggering $20 billion.

To have any chance of overcoming these penalty costs to make the program profitable, there remained tough challenges in effectively guiding the composite and all-electrical airplane through the rigorous certification process. This process would inevitably involve engineering changes along with the resulting manufacturing process changes as the factory workers came down the learning curve for efficiently manufacturing the airplane. Only this time, the learning curve results had to be fanned back out to the multitude of dispersed strategic partners that were building the various major components of the airplane. These changes required new manufacturing processes, new tooling, and additional training of the factory workers. And, indeed, many of the "fixes" had to be developed by engineers at the strategic partner sites rather than by Boeing engineers. The coordination and execution of all this posed unexpected and daunting challenges, to say the least. And to make matters worse, the program was still incurring serious supply chain and quality of work problems.

A host of additional design and manufacturing problems during the certification had worsened global supply chain problems. In December 2010 the *Seattle Times* reported on the problem-prone 787 and published a photograph of a growing number of unfinished 787s on the tarmac outside the Everett factory. One year after the successful maiden flight, twenty 787s stood on the tarmac with an estimated 140,000 "travelers"—that is, 140,000 work orders still to be completed to bring the twenty airplanes to completion.[27]

On August 26, 2011, U.S. Federal Aviation Administration (FAA) and European Air Safety Agency certified the 787, at last allowing airline deliveries to take place. The rather speedy certification of the 787 was not without controversy.

Boeing had become an influential force in Washington, D.C. President Barack Obama toured the 787 Everett Plant in 2009, and in March 2010 appointed Boeing CEO James McNerney to chair the president's export council. As reported by Dominic Rushe in *The Guardian* on January 18, 2013, former consultant and airline executive Robert Mann opined that Boeing's clout put pressure on the FAA to expedite approval for the Dreamliner, despite its radical design and manufacturing process."[28]

On September 25, 2011, the first 787 was delivered to Japan's ANA—three years behind schedule. The following month, the first 787 commercial airline flight carried passengers from Narita to Hong Kong. But the design and manufacturing problems were far from over. On December 5, 2012, the FAA ordered inspections of all 787s in service following reports of fuel leaks. In the same month, McNerney told media outlets that the problems were no greater than those experienced by other new Boeing airplanes such as the Boeing 777.

Still the problems persisted. Just a month later, on January 7, 2013, a fire broke out on a parked Japan Airlines 787 at Boston's Logan Airport—not the first smoke and fire experienced by 787s. And on January 16, 2013, the FAA issued an emergency airworthiness directive ordering all U.S.-based airlines to ground their Boeing 787s until modifications were made to the electrical systems to reduce the risk of batteries overheating or catching fire.

By January 17, 2013, all airlines had grounded the entire fleet of fifty Dreamliners that had been delivered. The FAA grounding of a fleet of airplanes had not happened since June 1979 when the McDonnell-Douglas DC-10s were grounded following an in-flight hydraulics failure that caused a widely publicized crash landing of a DC-10 in the Midwest.[29]

ANA airlines, which had taken the first delivery and had integrated a total of seventeen Dreamliners into its airline fleet, estimated that the cost to ANA of grounding the 787s exceeded $1 million per day. The FAA did not lift the grounding directive until April 19, 2013, some ninety-three days after it was issued. Counting ANA's daily cost of $1 million for grounding seventeen Dreamliners, we arrive at a cost per plane of about $5.4 million for this delay. Multiplying that amount by fifty (the total number of delivered 787s across all airlines) gives a total grounding cost to the airlines of some $270 million, which greatly overshadowed Boeing's $20 million cost in late delivery penalties.

Until the Logan Airport 787 battery fire and the subsequent grounding of all the 787s in service, McNerney had kept a low profile regarding the Dreamliner program and its problems. But now the crisis was fast eroding Boeing's long-term relationships with its airline customers. McNerney plunged directly into the problem with his outside scientific and technical staff and personally called on outside experts to assist. Still, it took ninety-three days to resolve the problem to the satisfaction of the FAA and return the 787 fleet to the skies

The critical question remains: How did this happen?

Did Boeing's CEO and board not know what was going on? If not, should they have? If they did, why didn't they take action to get the problems solved before they got so out of control? Where was board oversight to catch things like this and correct them?

WHAT HAD HAPPENED?

It seems that in a relatively short period—1997 to 2007—three CEOs launched Boeing into a downward tailspin. It wasn't a failure of vision or strategy; it was successive failures in execution.

The biggest failure of all was the failure to effectively integrate the McDonnell-Douglas culture into the Boeing company culture. It is important to remember that Condit's vision and the 2016 strategy made sense when articulated in 1996, and it still makes sense. Being a twenty-first-century aerospace industry leader required research (the space systems division for leading-edge research), the ability to apply that leading-edge research into potential commercial products (military defense one-off and/or limited production products), and mass production of commercial airplane products (the commercial airplanes division).

But the failure to integrate cultures spurred a dysfunctional power struggle between the McDonnell-Douglas and Boeing executives in the company and at board level, where McDonnell-Douglas executives and board members prevailed in influence. Moreover, there were many executive management failings. As a creator, Condit served Boeing well in creating the 2016 vision and strategy. He went on to serve Boeing well along with Allan Mulally in creating the plan for designing and manufacturing an industry game-changing commercial airplane. But at a time when Boeing needed more of a steward than a creator to execute the 2016 strategy, Condit became distracted and isolated as CEO, and as a result of the cumulative missteps at Boeing, the board finally asked for his resignation.

What should or could Condit have done differently? With hindsight, first off, he should have cleared away distractions. The lesson here is that today's CEOs hold leadership responsibility over thousands of people's lives and important global assets requiring minimum distractions: their responsibilities are more than a full-time job.

Second, Condit was still at Boeing during the board debate on simultaneously designing and manufacturing the Dreamliner with extensive global outsourcing, instead of first manufacturing it within Boeing's existing factories, and then embarking on the extensive outsourcing program. Again, in hindsight, the second, more cautious alternative would probably have been better. Even with Condit's compromised position at the time, he was still a respected Boeing leader, and he remained one of Boeing's prestigious legendary aerospace engineers.

Both past and sitting CEOs have unique and important perspectives about leading the corporation. Throughout Boeing's history, past CEOs had remained on the board to facilitate the transition to a successor CEO and retained respected leadership status in the corporation. This tradition continued during the twentieth century but fell into disuse in the twenty-first. Was that part of the reason that Boeing skipped a beat with the 787?

CEOs and boards should take a hard look at the pros and cons of continuity in the process of leadership transitions. The pros might well outweigh the cons in situations like Boeing's, where a smart but extremely ambitious strategy requires executive-level subject matter expertise for appropriate oversight and seasoned judgment for critical decisions.

Third, Condit should have been more persistent in sharing with his successor CEOs his unique perspective on the importance of IT as an important strategic resource. Condit's 2002 address at the MIT Sloan School's Fiftieth Anniversary certainly reflected a thoughtful understanding about the key role of strategic IT. Despite not growing up with IT (being a digital immigrant), Condit noted the importance of IT strategy, particularly given the increasingly pervasive role of the Internet and its potential for making information transparency a reality. Because of IT-enabled information transparency, almost everyone knew about the seriousness of 787 problems and delivery delays. In this transparent environment, Boeing's credibility suffered when company executives tried to keep the information about the delays under wraps. It was dangerous and futile for the Boeing leadership to try and hide such critical information as the problems that delayed the delivery of the 787.

Even worse, in a time of unprecedented transitions in communications technology, Boeing's senior leaders failed to fully leverage IT-enabled real-time communications to keep all stakeholders in the 787 Dreamliner program informed on the latest information regarding the execution problems for the new airplane. Boeing's global strategic partners had high stakes as well as important influence on the effective execution of the 787 program, but without the newest IT-enhanced communications capabilities, the mission-critical coordination efforts seemed less than adequate for such an extremely complex endeavor. Condit had a good sense of what needed to happen to use Boeing's IT capabilities in this manner but did not seem to persuade his colleagues to adopt the same perspective.

The Boeing board of directors showed similar shortcomings. By the time the board was forced to act, the power struggle between the Boeing and McDonnell-Douglas executives and board members had already played out, and the McDonnell-Douglas contingent had prevailed. While the prestigious Boeing name still appeared on the buildings, the McDonnell-Douglas executives flooded into the top echelons, and their influence and corporate culture had a major influence on the executive team and the board of directors. Some cynics described the acquisition as a reverse takeover whereby "McDonnell Douglas acquired Boeing with Boeing's own money!"

Personal motivations and money were not necessarily aligned with the health of the company. Executive management bonuses were based on performance share grants, which converted to common stock triggered by increases in share price. Financial engineering programs encouraged shedding assets and increased reliance on outsourcing. Assets of the commercial airplane group declined to $9.8 billion in 2000 compared to $11 billion in 1998.

Other programs focused on increasing profits by cutting expenses. R&D expenses for commercial airplanes were cut from $1 billion in 1998 to $574 million in 2000; capital expenditures for the group during the same period were reduced to $237 million from $754 million.

A shareholder suit claimed that Boeing used "accounting tricks to cover up the assembly line shutdown." Boeing paid $92.5 million to settle the suit. Wall Street analysts became highly critical of Condit's performance, and at an internal Boeing meeting, a contrite Condit graded himself "F" on his own performance leading to the factory shutdown.

A survey of employee morale was 69 percent positive in 1998, but it had plummeted to 31 percent positive by the next year.[30] The clash of corporate cultures was a huge factor in the decline.

Airbus was undeterred in eating away at Boeing's leading commercial airplane manufacturing market share. By 2003 Airbus was producing more commercial airplanes than Boeing and had amassed a larger backlog of orders to surpass Boeing and become the market leader.

The restructured Boeing board would go onto elect the previous McDonnell-Douglas CEO to succeed Condit. As Boeing CEO, Stonecipher clashed with Alan Mullaly, CEO of Commercial Airplane, about the 787 new airplane program. Stonecipher held considerable sway, and the board approved the 787 program, ostensibly shifting major financial risk to an unprecedented extensive network of global outsourcers. The unintended result was that Boeing retained operational risk, and when the operational risk actually materialized, Boeing also realized the financial risk—billions in delivery penalty costs and billions in rework costs, not to mention the billions of costs that their airline customers incurred from grounded airplanes because of safety concerns. A mere fifteen months later, Harry Stonecipher was replaced.

Choosing Stonecipher's successor came down to a two-horse race between board member Jim McNerney (known as the GE guy) and insider Alan Mulally. The board chose McNerney. Almost immediately, Mulally left.

Boeing continued to operate with a fractured culture whereby at the top, the twentieth-century GE model of managing by the numbers was now deeply entrenched to the detriment of the Boeing culture. At the middle and lower levels, the Boeing culture prevailed in commercial airplane, and for the most part the McDonnell-Douglas culture prevailed in defense. The space business units largely disappeared along with the space market. The Boeing Leadership Center in St. Louis continued to run programs to integrate the two cultures, but as a McDonnell-Douglas-established facility, it retained its historical bias in running the Center as well as designing programs and selecting instructors. The instructors mostly consisted of practicing executives from McNerney's executive team.

McNerney carried on CEO leadership of Boeing, which continued to be "stuck in the middle" by largely keeping Boeing's existing commercial airplane and defense businesses operating as they had been. The original goals of transforming the organization by implementing the 787 Dreamliner program were overwhelmed by the challenges of debugging the new airplane and simultaneously scaling 787 manufacturing in order to foresee breakeven and profitability on the distant horizon. Lost in the process were further efforts to execute the 2016 strategy of transforming the existing businesses to realize the vision of becoming primarily a complex systems integrator.

McNerney and the board lost ground as Boeing dropped from being viewed as one of the best-managed corporations to one of the worst. Allowing the mixed Boeing and McDonnell-Douglas corporate cultures to coexist was confusing to all of the workers and likely nonsustainable. And with five new board members added during McNerney's tenure as CEO, Boeing's board had come under attack for not providing the oversight of the CEO leadership that would have been necessary to turn the situation around.

The catastrophe of the 787 fleet grounding in January 2013 might have been a wake-up call and a catalyst for McNerney to apply his leadership capabilities to revitalize the execution of the downward spiraling strategic 787 program. At the Paris Airshow, in a CNBC interview on June 17, 2013, McNerney directly talked about the 787 battery crisis along with Boeing's business, challenges, and future prospects.[31]

While the statement that company culture is everything in corporate transformation is an overstatement, culture plays an ever-more central role. Factors such as organizational structure, leadership, and technology are important, and the interaction among these factors is also important. In chapter 5 we turn to the role of technology in management by wire.

NOTES

1. The Moonshine Group came about as an initiative of Boeing's 2016 strategy. My colleagues and I were so impressed with the work of the Moonshine Group that we wrote a field case on the structure and processes of the group. See Austin, R., Nolan, R., and O'Donnell, S., "The Boeing Company Moonshine Group," Harvard Business School Case #607–130, April 9, 2007.
2. Harvard Business School video of Lou Gerstner speaking to the HBS Class of 1995 at HBS in the fall of 1994. Lou Gerstner was a 1965 Harvard MBA and sponsored the development of a HBS case study on IBM's turnaround, which

was authored by myself and Professor Robert Austin. Gerstner addressed the MBA classes of 2002 (November 20, 2002) and 2003 and continued to speak on IBM's transformation at HBS with his previous Senior Vice President of Strategy Bruce Herrald, who had been appointed a HBS faculty Lecturer.

3. R. L. Nolan Skype video interview with Phil Condit, January 12, 2010. Phil shared his perspectives with me on the nature and importance of corporate culture after reading my early draft for this book, and engaging in an hour-long Skype video interchange in 2010 on the Boeing corporate culture.

4. The cost of the part to fix the switch was estimated at less than $1 per car in documents that GM submitted to Congress.

5. Krisher, Tom, and Gordon, Marcy, "Mary Barra Tries to Assure Congress GM Has Changed Its Ways, but Old Culture Looms Large," Associated Press, April 1, 2014, www.news1130.com/2014/04/02/mary-barra-tries-to-assure-congress-gm-has-changed-its-ways-but-old-culture-looms-large/.

6. My student MBA experience at the University of Washington was somewhat similar to Gerstner's, but with one significant difference. My Organization Behavior course was taught by Professor Borje Saxberg, a through and through Swedish national, who every year until his retirement from the faculty of the University of Washington returned to his farm in Sweden during his teaching off-months. Professor Saxberg had a more European approach to teaching organization behavior and culture, and his HBO course was one of the most popular courses for those in my MBA class. Professor Saxberg was still actively teaching when I returned to the University of Washington in 2003, and we engaged in a number of long discussions on culture and Boeing's corporate culture.

7. Satya Nadella, July 10, 2014 email to all Microsoft employees, "Starting FY15—Bold Ambition & Our Core," www.microsoft.com/en-us/news/ceo/index.html, accessed by author on July 11, 2014.

8. Tu, Janet I., "Microsoft CEO Satya Nadella Lays out 'Unique Strategy,'" *Seattle Times*, July 11, 2014, p. 1.

9. Moeller, Sara B., Schlingemann, Frederik P., and Stulz, Rene M., "Wealth Destruction on a Massive Scale?" National Bureau of Economic Research Working Paper No. 10200, 2004.

10. Three hundred eighty-eight DC-10s had been sold, and the DC-10 had an average safety record over its life.

11. Soon after Condit's move of Boeing headquarters from Seattle to Chicago, he was interviewed on September 2, 2001, for an article appearing in the *Chicago Tribune*, "True Confession: Boeing Among GE Copycats": "Someone asked if there's another company Condit thinks of as a model for Boeing's changes. He named: General Electric, everyone's favorite $130 billion colossus. . . . 'There are certain elements of GE that are clearly a model,' Condit said. 'The move to Chicago was part of a GE-inspired decision to get headquarters away from operations. Boeing's newish St. Louis training facility replicates a GE concept. . . . We shamelessly stole from GE," Condit confessed.' See "Boeing to fly from Seattle," by Chris Isidoro, staff writer, CNN Money, March 21, 2001, accessed by author on September 15, 2014, url: http://money.cnn.com/2001/03/21/companies/boeing/

12. Boeing was awarded a U.S. Air Force $20 billion tanker contract to purchasing twenty Boeing KC-767 tankers, and leasing twenty more, to replace the aging KC-135 U.S. military tanker fleet. In December 2003, the Pentagon froze the contract while an investigation of allegations of corruption by one if its former procurement staffers, Darleen Druyun (who had become a Boeing executive in January 2003) was carried out. Druyun was terminated from Boeing and pled

guilty of criminal wrongdoing and was sentenced to nine months in jail for "negotiating a job with Boeing at the same time she was involved in contracts with the company." Additional fallout included the termination of Boeing's Chief Financial Officer, Michael Sears, and subsequently the resignation of Condit. Boeing paid $615 million in fines to the U.S. government. In January 2006, and the contract was formally canceled.

13. See Slater, Robert, *Jack Welch and the GE Way* (New York: McGraw-Hill, 1999).

14. By 2003, it had been more than a decade since Boeing had last been involved in a new commercial airplane program—the last new airplane program was the Boeing 777. In light of the McDonnell acquisition and Airbus's inroads into Boeing's commercial airplane business, some were questioning whether Boeing intended to leave the commercial airplane business and become solely a defense contractor.

15. The first was Harry Stonecipher, who came with the Boeing acquisition of McDonnell-Douglas. All the other CEOs during Boeings near one hundred years as a corporation had extensive experience at Boeing in various senior executive or board positions.

16. CEO Jack Welch established at Crotonville an executive education campus along with professional instructors who worked with GE top executives, including Jack Welch, to deliver tailored executive education to the management ranks of GE. GE's Crotonville was one of the most aggressive ExecEd programs of any corporation and was highly successful in creating a shared corporate culture. While the GE Crotonville program was staffed by trained administrator-educators, the curriculum was primarily delivered by top executives of GE.

17. Reported by Tuttle, Rich, Aero*space Daily & Defense Report*, 215 no. 1 (New York: McGraw-Hill, July 1, 2005).

18. Millares Bolt, Kristen, *Seattle Post Intelligencer*, July 1, 2005.

19. *Ibid.*

20. For a detailed analysis of the costly series of delivery delays of the 787, see the case study "Build to Performance—Boeing 787 Dreamliner," prepared and copyrighted 2010 by doctoral student Xin Xu and Professor Yao Zhao, Rutgers Business School.

21. Gates, Dominic, "Boeing Unveils 787 Dreamliner in Worldwide Production," *Seattle Times*, July 7, 2007. Photograph by Mike Siegel *Seattle Times*. The 787 shown in the photo was Plane 1, and it was far from a complete airplane, and would never fly. The 787 that would be successfully certified would be Plane 3.

22. Society of Professional Engineering Employees in Aerospace.

23. Scott Carson interview by Joseph Weber of *Aviation Week*, January 19, 2009.

24. Pat Shanahan would subsequently be replaced by Scott Fancher in late 2008. And then in February 2012, Fancher was replaced by long-time Boeing employee and factory manager, Larry Loftis.

25. Pat Shanahan would subsequently be replaced with Scott Fancher in late 2008. See Peter Pae, staff writer *Los Angeles Times* "Boeing Again Delays First 787 Delivery," January 17, 2008. Accessed by the the author on September 15, 2014: www.latimes.com/local/la-fi-boeing17jan17-story.html

And then in February 2012, Fancher was replaced by long time Boeing employee and factory manager, Larry Loftis.

26. Plane 1 had to be scrapped due to the cost of dismantling the partially finished airplane and rebuilding it to a functional 787 airplane.

27. Gates, "Dreamliner Woes Pile Up," *Seattle Times*, December 18, 2010.

28. Rushe, Dominic, "Why Boeing's 787 Dreamliner Was a Nightmare Waiting to Happen" *The Guardian*, January 18, 2013, www.theguardian.com/business/2013/jan/18/boeing-787-dreamliner-grounded, accessed by author on December 11, 2013.
29. The FAA DC-10 grounding came after a Turkish Airlines DC-10 crashed over Paris in 1974 after a cargo door blew off, killing 346 people and then, in May 1979, an American Airlines DC-10 crashed during takeoff in Chicago and killed 293 people. In June 1979, the FAA grounded the DC-10 commercial airline fleet.
30. For an extensive research report and analysis of the changing Boeing employees and their perceptions about the Boeing Company, see Greenberg, Edward S., Grunberg, Leon, Moore, Sarah, and Sikora, Patricia B., *Turbulence: Boeing and the State of the American Workers and Managers* (New Haven and London: Yale University Press, 2010).
31. See the video of James McNerney's June 17, 2013, CNBC interview Boeing CEO: Belvedere, Matthew J., "'Highly Confident' in 787 Battery Fix," CNBC's "Squawk Box," www.cnbc.com/id/100820102, accessed by author on December 14, 2013.

BIBLIOGRAPHY

Greenberg, Edward S., Grunberg, Leon, Moore, Sarah, and Sikora, Patricia B., *Turbulence: Boeing and the State of the American Workers and Managers* (New Haven and London: Yale University Press, 2010).
Moeller, Sara B., Schlingemann, Frederik P., and Stulz, Rene M., "Wealth Destruction on a Massive Scale?" National Bureau of Economic Research Working Paper No. 10200, 2004.
Slater, Robert. *Jack Welch and the GE Way* (New York: McGraw-Hill, 1999).

5 Managing by Wire

It is rather ironic that Boeing, which introduced the jet age of commercial flight in the 1950s with its successful Boeing 707, went on to internalize the concept of "fly by wire" in its family of jet airplanes but did not extend the concept to "manage by wire" to run its far-flung operations. The irony increases in that Phil Condit not only embraced "fly by wire" for his Boeing 777 airliner but also made frequent public pronouncements about the company's vision of IT-enabled networks for the military as well as for the modern corporation.

Today, "heads up" displays in cockpits augment a pilot's ability to fly and land jet airplanes safely. Pilots receive automatic updates and warnings about selected information such as in-flight geography below, incoming weather, and dangerously close oncoming airplanes. And when the pilot responds by making a decision, it's the computer systems that translate the command into the thousands of detailed orders that orchestrate the airplane's behavior in real time—faster and more efficiently than the pilot could ever do alone.

As explained to me by Phil Condit,[1] the company assumes that there is no such thing as pilot error—that is, that pilots are an integral part of the system for flying airplanes. Boeing's Airplane-on-the-Ground (AOG) program immediately deploys a team of Boeing experts to investigate critical incidents or accidents. If the pilot makes a decision in flight that causes a crash, the going-in assumption is that there was an airplane systems problem (again, airplane systems include pilots). Pilots undergo rigorous training and continuous maintenance skill training, just as other parts of the system require routine maintenance and upgrades.

The early concept of recognizing commercial airplane pilots as integral to the planes' flight systems and designing those systems to be pilot fail-safe systems was a logical step in Boeing's strategy. Without this integrating concept of humans and computers, commercial flight never would have advanced to the level that it has, including the incredible safety record maintained during the millions of commercial airplane flights every year.

This early insight makes it even more difficult to understand why Boeing hasn't applied this same approach to develop integrated manager-computer systems to meet the challenges of guiding the modern corporation. Perhaps part of the reason can be gleaned from the stages of corporation growth as discussed in chapter 1—that is, fully integrating IT into corporations is an advanced-stage phenomenon mostly taking place in the twenty-first century.

RETOOLING THE ORGANIZATION
FOR MANAGING BY WIRE

Steve Haeckel and I introduced our original analogy for the strategic opportunity enabled by IT in our 1993 *Harvard Business Review* article, "Managing by Wire."[2] We started by describing the early and innovative use of IT in a relatively simple cookie business: Mrs. Fields.[3] Debbi Fields opened a cookie store in Palo Alto, California, and successfully sold home-made cookies from her own recipes. In 1978, she opened her second cookie store in San Francisco (forty-five miles away from her first store in Palo Alto) and faced the problem of maintaining her hands-on management style for running the second store. Her husband, Randy, was a skilled computer professional and worked with Debbi to develop software that would help run remote stores the way that Debbi ran the Palo Alto store. Eight hundred stores later, the management of Mrs. Fields stores used Randy's software to issue instructions and advice to each store manager.

Each morning, local store managers projected sales for the day and entered information into a personal computer including day of the week, season, and local weather conditions. The PC software analyzed the information and responded with hourly directions on what to do to meet the day's objectives. These directions included how many batches of different cookies to mix and bake; how to adjust the directions as the day's customer buying patterns unfolded; and when to offer free samples (referred to as "chumming").[4]

Mrs. Fields retail cookie stores were relatively simple businesses characterized by an innovative vision but also high turnover of store managers. Randy's software hardwired Mrs. Fields's vision and management approach in each store. Several principles explain why the management by wire approach worked. First, the concept of "how we do things around here" was well understood—that is, a conviction that quality must be centrally controlled. The effect of the IT applications was to facilitate inculcation of the corporate culture and the day-to-day workings of the stores.

A second principle was information sharing: information would be shared between central management and local store managers. The effect here was to facilitate culture and communications among managers and workers throughout geographically dispersed business units.

The Mrs. Fields hard-wired approach to managing by wire was analogous to the autopilot system of an airplane, both of which have elements of rigidity. The drawbacks of rigidity in the software systems designed for U.S. cookie stores became obvious as Mrs. Fields expanded into Europe and

Asia with customers coming from different cultures and tastes. Similarly, the rigidity of a hardwired autopilot system can become problematic as an airplane goes through different flying conditions without the intervention of a pilot.

To be useful in today's fast-changing environment, managing by wire must go beyond hardwired business processes; it must also incorporate the flexibility of organizational learning. As with Boeing's fly by wire concept for commercial jet airplanes, the organization and people must operate as one integrated system. This concept has been incorporated into the U.S. Air Force training and evaluation of fighter jet pilots.[5] The training includes the OODA learning loop: observation, orientation, decision, and action. The loop is a continuous cycle of learning. Similarly, the four functions essential to an adaptive, successful management by wire organization are sensing, interpreting, deciding, and acting.

Wal-Mart's system for store replenishment of Wrangler Jeans offers an example of integrating IT and people as a single system with organizational learning. Every evening, Wal-Mart transmits millions of characters of data about its store sales of Wrangler Jeans to Wrangler. The two companies share the data and IT application for interpreting the meaning of the data. They also share the applications that act on that interpretation to send specific quantities of sizes and colors of jeans to stores from a network of warehouses. Wal-Mart and Wrangler continuously learn and adapt together as the people and software track sales through new fashion seasons and pricing patterns.[6]

In this way, an intelligent corporation uses IT to integrate how it senses and interprets "what's going on out there" with its internal dynamic learning about "how we do things around here" to build a capacity for rapid, effective responses to ever-changing markets.[7]

With hundreds of millions in revenue and tens of thousands of employees operating around the globe, CEOs and their executive teams can't track everything that happens or coordinate millions of elements in a timely, coherent response. Indeed, the modern corporations of the twentieth century attained their size and geographic spread by adapting decentralized functional hierarchies to serve diverse business units.

FROM HIERARCHIES TO NETWORKS

However, by the late twentieth century, IT had begun to enable a more efficient and agile alternative to the large functional hierarchical structures of older corporations. Such hierarchies and their chain-of-command communication structures were designed for a relatively stable "make-and-sell" business environment, which was increasingly becoming obsolete.

The pioneers in developing the newer forms included a number of corporations in the relatively young computer industry, such as Cisco and Apple, as they substituted IT-enabled networks for hierarchy. The main advantages of the new form came from increased cost efficiency through centralizing redundant functions and the ability to shift the speed of resource allocation from annual and quarterly budgetary events to real-time events.

Traditional large corporations like Boeing were also migrating to the IT-enabled networks. Boeing's 2016 strategy was conceived with that goal in mind. In my interviews with Phil Condit, he clearly envisioned achieving the 2016 strategy of becoming a large systems aerospace integrator as enabled by network-era IT technologies. The Dreamliner airplane program, with its global partnerships and interconnecting technologies, was also originally seen as a product-driven spearhead for transforming all of Boeing to a twenty-first-century industry leader.

It is well known that organizational change is hard. It is also well known that major organizational change is significantly helped along when corporations face a major crisis. This is especially true when the necessary change requires moving from a large and established decentralized, divisionalized functional hierarchy to a more efficient IT-enabled network organizational structure.

A corporate organizational structure is designed to leverage the dominant technology of an economy for carrying out work. The dominant technologies of the nineteenth century into the twentieth century were energy-based technologies: water wheels, electricity, steam engines, internal combustion engines, and ram-jet engines. These technologies enabled the transition to the next stage of economic development, whereby the majority of workers went from doing farm work to industrial, or factory work. The tool-based agrarian economy did not disappear but instead grew by applying energy technologies to increase production—that is, mechanizing the farm, so that agriculture no longer required the majority of a country's workforce, but more like one-twentieth of the workforce. This freed up the majority of the workforce for leveraging the emerging energy technologies to new industries and innovative work processes—that is, the mass production stage of twentieth-century corporations' growth, which resulted in myriad new products including appliances, cars, machines, and jet airplanes.

None of this would have been possible without the complementary invention of the vertically integrated functional hierarchy to carry out industrial work. Adapted from the church and military, this historical structure enabled large numbers of people to be organized into a hierarchy of groups working toward a commonly shared goal. The military used a building block structure in which squads of seven to ten soldiers led by a squad leader were combined into platoons (two to four squads), companies (three to four platoons), battalions (three to five companies), brigades (three or more battalions), divisions (three brigades), corps (two to three divisions), and field army (three to five corps). The chain of command led upward from the squad leader to the top general, who held responsibility for leading the overall multilevel hierarchy. The span of control at each level, beginning with squad leaders, reflected the number of soldiers a leader could effectively manage in carrying out orders. Strategic planning and communication originated from the top and filtered down to specific tasks to be executed at each level, and results were communicated back up the hierarchy. This structure, which incorporated military terms such as "line and staff," "chain of command," and "span of control" to identify many specific positions and groups, became the prevailing organizational form for factories and most other businesses in the twentieth century.

As we traced the evolution of the organizational structure at the Boeing Corporation, the functional hierarchy first appeared as an integrated vertical hierarchy designed to build a complex airplane. The vertically integrated organization included design (Boeing Engineering), parts fabrication (Boeing Manufacturing), major components such as engines (Pratt Whitney), assembly into major structural components and final airplane assembly (Boeing Manufacturing), training (Boeing mechanics and pilot training), and customer service (United Airlines).

By 1934, the hugely successful design, manufacture, and commercialization of Boeing's airplanes began to clash with the U.S. government's interest in encouraging competition and avoiding monopolies. So the government brought an antitrust lawsuit against Boeing to force it to break up its integrated structure by divesting both Pratt Whitney and United Airlines. Similar directives forced other successful vertically integrated corporations such as Standard Oil, Great American and Pacific Tea Company (A&P), RCA (Radio Corporation of America), and IBM to restructure and/or divest major businesses as well.

World War II would be the crisis that resulted in Boeing and many other companies mastering mass production of complex industrial products; propelling these corporations first into very large, billion-dollar revenue corporations; and then further into multibillion-dollar corporations. Rudimentary information technology was used to meet the demands for information in coordinating the increasingly sophisticated operations of mass production. The early forms included typewriters, the telegraph, the telephone, and then the punched card and early machines of IBM and Remington Rand (ADP—Automated Data Processing).[8]

BOEING: LEAN MANUFACTURING BEFORE LEAN MANUFACTURING

At its peak, Boeing's Seattle Plant 2 built sixteen B-17s in a twenty-four-hour period. Figure 5.1 shows the sixteen completed B-17s on the Boeing Field tarmac on April 30, 1944.

Figure 5.1   Sixteen Boeing B-17s Manufactured within Twenty-Four Hours

Total Boeing production of B-17s amounted to 6,981. With collaboration from Boeing, Lockheed and Douglas factories produced another 5,745 B-17s.[9]

The B-17 (Model 299) prototype, financed entirely by Boeing, went from design to first flight test (July 28, 1935) in less than twelve months. Upon roll-out, a newspaper man in attendance cried out, "It's a flying fortress"—a name that stuck. The B-17 was a low-wing monoplane that combined aerodynamic features of the XB-15 giant bomber and the Model 247 transport. It was the first Boeing military aircraft with a flight deck instead of an open cockpit. As revolutionary as the B-17 was as a modern military airplane, equally revolutionary were the innovations in the manufacturing of the B-17s including an advanced B-17 factory system housed in a state-of-art factory designated as Plant 2. See Figure 5.2.

The advanced manufacturing system consisted of an important set of management processes: work breakdown, build to print, modularization, workflow, machine tool integration, coordinated build teams, supply chain and outsourcing, and engineering change orders.

Figure 5.2   Boeing Plant 2: "Lean Manufacturing" of B-17s

Work Breakdown

The work breakdown structure started with a conceptual design and an art-ist's rendition of the airplane, which incorporated the desired performance characteristics and goals at a high level. From the conceptual design, the air-plane was broken down into its major components such as wings, fuselage, and engines (now often referred to as Tier 1 components), and from there into detailed engineering designs and drawings for all the parts in the entire airplane, and for the machine tools to make the parts.

George Schairer (1913–2004), legendary Boeing engineer, pioneered this approach. He also was a talented artist and model airplane builder, and he used those skills to communicate effectively with senior Air Force mili-tary leaders.[10] Schairer's work helped to convince the Wright Patterson Air Force staff to shift from investing in turbo-jet engine technology for the B-52 bomber prototype to swept-wing ram-jet engine propulsion.

Build to Print

A modern commercial airplane consists of 3 to 6 million parts. The design is initiated within a relatively small team. Once the conceptual design is decided, the work processes are designed. Next, the detailed engineering specifies the dimensions, materials, and function of each part. Then manufacturing engineering undertakes tooling necessary to produce each of the parts. At this point, the relatively small team explodes to hundreds, if not thousands, of engineers to develop the detailed drawings for the millions of parts and the machine tool drawings necessary to produce the parts. Since the B-17, the drawing process has changed from hand-drafting to computer-generated CAD/CAM (computer-aided design/computer-aided manufacturing) drawings. Today, many of the computer-generated drawings can be directly loaded into numerically controlled machines automating the manufacture of parts.[11] This process of creating computer databases for parts and tooling early on led Boeing to establish operations in global sites such as Moscow (i.e., Boeing's Moscow Design Center) to supplement the company's internal engineering design and manufacturing capabilities. The expanded capability was essential to support the extensive outsourcing among Boeing's strategic global partners involved in designing and building the Dreamliner.

Modularization

Modularization is the process of grouping the parts into subassemblies cascading into major groupings of subassemblies building up to Tier 1 major components that flow into final assembly on the factory floor to a completed airplane.

The integration of modules is an art form that involves a process of designing as much as possible into a module and creating a standard interface for connecting one module to others. Improving the module design continues to evolve during the process of efficiently learning to build the airplane on the assembly line.

The B-17 worked modules up to seven major Tier 1 components: right inboard wing, left inboard wing, forward third of fuselage, middle third of fuselage, aft third of fuselage and tail, right outboard wing, and left outboard wing. These seven Tier 1 components were then integrated and bolted together by final assembly teams. This process was continually refined and improved and is roughly the process that was extended to global design and manufacture of the Boeing 787.

Workflow

Workflow processes were continuously revised, as the Boeing teams accumulated experience. Production engineers roamed and observed manufacturing and interacted with mechanics to continuously improve the efficiency of the manufacturing process. With the advent of the 737 moving line, extensive use of carts on wheels improved the speed at which modules moved from work group to work group during the build/assembly process.

Machine Tool Integration

Machine tools were designed for efficiency and to maintain the high level of tolerances necessary to build high altitude, high performance, and reliable airplanes. Emphasis was on building small, portable tooling versus large, expensive and inflexible machine tools referred to as "monuments."

Coordinated Work Teams

The workers who built the B-17 in Plant 2 numbered about 33,000. During World War II, half of Plant 2 workers were women drawn into the workforce, taking on their first jobs outside the home. Teams of twenty to twenty-five directly carried out the work on the factory floor according to clearly illustrated instructions of no more than two pages long for each task as designed by production engineers.

The team's work was paced by wind-up clock timers. The process was similar to a disciplined professional sports team knowing their jobs and places on the field where they needed to be during each play of the game. As the work was carried out by each team, a visible board holding cards showed the progress of the work for each module by airplane number and could be used for all the workers to see when work fell behind plan. In those cases, cross-trained workers from other team members would be called upon to get the work back on schedule. Production engineers roved the factory floor and acted as expediters and coaches to the teams.

From the early days to the present, the efficient working of the teams has entailed training, careful make-up of the teams, well-designed and well-timed work packages for each of the teams, clearly illustrated instructions for the tasks of each team member, and cooperation among the factory workers and the production engineers to continuously innovate and improve the workflow.

The innovative construction and use of teams by Boeing was carried forward during the design and manufacture of the Boeing 777. Under the leadership of Phil Condit, Boeing created Design, Build, and Support Teams (DBST).

Supply Chain and Outsourcing

Managing the supply chain of millions of parts flowing into successively more complete subassemblies was one of the most difficult and elusive processes of advanced mass production, and it has become even more complicated today with global manufacturing.

Once the work breakdown structure was established and detailed engineering drawings completed, a manufacturing schedule was decided. Next, the millions of detailed engineering drawing were fanned out to the supply chain, some companies owned by Boeing, some not.

To meet the aggressive B-17 production schedule, Boeing began outsourcing part manufacturing to supplier factories of 250 employees or less within a fifty-mile radius of Plant 2. Point of use inventories were maintained and referred to as the "Fuller Brush Salesman System."[12] If a mechanic ran out of a part, he was authorized to telephone the supplier directly for a timely replenishment. When a supplier ran into quality or schedule problems in manufacturing a part, Boeing maintained skilled swat teams to "parachute in" to assist the supplier. This process was learned by Boeing early on after the 1934 antitrust divesture of their Pratt Whitney business unit.

The airplane engine is one of the most critical systems of a modern commercial airplane. Early on, Boeing was forced to learn to work with their airplane engine strategic partner in close collaboration for design, manufacturing, airplane certification, and service. This learning provided Boeing with a unique capability that has since become refined as an essential capability for successful twenty-first-century corporations.

Outsourcing expanded geographically to national outsourcing, and from the second half of the twentieth century into the twenty-first, to global outsourcing. The 787 program significantly extended the concept of outsourcing to design as well as manufacturing in engaging strategic outsourcing partners around the world.

Boeing's supply chain management evolved from a highly controlled internal process, expanded to include regional suppliers, and finally included global partners involving an "extended organization" (a term coined by Cisco Systems) with sophisticated use of IT-enabled systems.

Vertically integrated corporate structures were common in the twentieth century, but they have continued to evolve into virtually integrated extended organizations with outside suppliers doing more and more in designing and building parts up into subassemblies. The more modern term, "outsourcing," is now used to describe horizontalization of industries into standalone corporations for designing and building subassemblies such as jet engines, fuselages, and wings for commercial airplanes.

To coordinate the increasingly complex supply chains of parts and subassemblies coming together, IT systems continue to evolve and extend outsourcing possibilities. But without strategic vision for the development and use of those IT systems to extend through the supply chain, Boeing missed the opportunity to head off part hoarding and shortages throughout the outsourcer network, thus exacerbating the costly delivery delays for the 787.

Engineering Change Orders

The engineering change order (ECO) is one of the most important, and often most contentious, processes in building a commercial airplane—as it has been for many other mass produced complex products such as automobiles. The ECO process attempts to balance the latest learnings and innovations against risk and cost implications. The ECO process continues from the time that the first detailed drawings are developed for a commercial airplane all the way through the manufacturing, flight test, and lifecycle of the program.

The magnitude and the detail are staggering. Perpetual inventories of all of the millions of parts on in-service commercial airplanes must be constantly maintained and updated. If an essential part on one airplane is found to be defective, the airplane inventories are checked to determine which other airplanes have that part, a replacement program is worked out, and then all the defective parts are replaced. And of course, careful maintenance records are kept for each airplane to ensure that the inventory of parts on the airplane is kept current.

With war-time and the use of B-17s in direct combat, managing ECOs took on a direct life-and-death import for the pilots and crews, and the manufacturing teams honed the process as close to perfection as possible. Completed B-17s were transported to the European war theater immediately after manufacturing and entered into combat. Very advanced, fast, highly maneuverable German fighter airplanes shot down many of the early B-17s. Rapid analysis of the B-17s' vulnerabilities led to a continuous stream of corrections via ECOs.

Boeing's Plant 2 balanced the need to make engineering changes in response to combat experience with the need for production efficiency by developing a system for making ECOs on a block of B-17s. Identical B-17s were produced in blocks of twenty to two hundred. ECOs were grouped and made to an entire block of B-17s in a manner that would minimize disruption to continuous production. The efficiency of the system was illustrated by the first production B-17E, with four hundred ECOs, which was test flown the day after the last B-17E was delivered.[13] Boeing made major improvements in the ECO process that led to the successful completion of the B-17G in record time.

During the second half of the twentieth century, Japanese innovators rediscovered the elements of this success at Plant 2, which they refined and relabeled "lean manufacturing," sometimes referred to as the Toyota Production System (TPS).

FROM PULSE ASSEMBLY LINES TO CONTINUOUSLY MOVING ASSEMBLY LINES

Boeing leadership continued to have faith in the efficiency of their factories until 1997, at which time Airbus aggressively priced their A-320 airplane lower than the Boeing 737. Boeing responded by lowering the price of the 737.

The 737 order book rebounded. But when Boeing attempted to increase production in its Renton 737 factory to meet the increased demand, chaos resulted, and the entire 737 assembly line had to be shut down to regain control. Boeing CEO Phil Condit removed their Renton 737 factory manager, but the root problem was not with the factory manager; the Boeing factory simply had fallen behind the competition and was no longer the most efficient commercial airplane manufacturer.

Prior to 1999, the Renton 737 plant was a pulse line, or station-to-station line, similar to the Plant 2 737 line I experienced in 1967. Figure 5.3 shows the 737 Renton factory in 1982.[14]

Note the inventory of parts stacked around the assembly line stations waiting to be installed. The slanted line is work-in-process 737s that were assembled at their respective work stations during the day and evening shifts, and then moved with an overhead crane to the next sequential work stations during the night shift.

The pulse assembly line dictated that planes be moved during times planned. If work was not accomplished by the time the plane was supposed to move, in most cases the airplane was moved anyway, and "traveler work" initiated. Traveler work was to be avoided almost at all costs since it cut into profitability due to inefficiencies in doing work on an airplane out of sequence. Management and workers dreaded seeing unfinished airplanes rolled onto the tarmac, not only because the traveler work

Figure 5.3   Boeing 737 Pulse Line

would have to be done out of sequence, in an ad hoc manner, but also because the extent of remedial work was exposed for all to see outside the factory.

I personally witnessed this serious problem in 1967 when the 737 manufacturing line was overwhelmed with ECOs leading to a hoard of unfinished 737s pushed out of Plant 2 and lined up on the tarmac of Boeing Field. The out-of-sequence work led to mechanics on ladders removing the windshields of the unfinished 737s and working on the cockpit ECOs. The awkwardness and expense of this problem was all too obvious.

THE COST STRUCTURE CRISIS

In scaling Boeing to accommodate the coordinated management tasks of simultaneously building a family of commercial airplanes, the integrated functional organization including its factories was "divisionalized" by product, by geography, and by functions (e.g., manufacturing and sales).

The Boeing Corporation was first divisionalized by business, then further decentralized by products within business divisions (and within product divisions by function). The advantage of the decentralized organizational structure was to facilitate focused management on the individual requirements of products. The disadvantage was duplication of functional units in each product unit, causing redundant cost creep.

The cost creep problem for Boeing continued as lean manufacturing techniques improved. Boeing experienced a slowly realized, self-evident truth: "all products become commodity-like over time." What was perhaps proprietary information associated with Boeing's competitive cost advantage had diffused with time and as people changed jobs, new entrants entered the marketplace, competition became heated up through new manufacturing processes and innovations; both costs manufacturing and product prices fell. This is what happened to Boeing by 1997, which spurred Boeing to catch up with competitor Airbus by transforming their traditional airplane manufacturing to a more modern continuous moving line. By 2002, Boeing had implemented the first continuously moving assembly line for a modern commercial airliner. The moving line shown in Figure 5.4 allowed 737s to be finally assembled in eleven days compared to the twenty-two days required on the pulse assembly line.[15]

Note from Figure 5.4 that that the moving line continuously flowed final assembly through the workstations at two inches per minute. Large barn doors the length of the factory on both sides allowed suppliers to progressively "feed" the moving line. "Kitting carts" on rollers can be seen staged along the line, which contained both parts and tools necessary to perform tasks at each work station. Finally, manufacturing engineers were housed on the second floor of the line with office windows overlooking the entire line

Figure 5.4   Boeing 737 Moving Line

including flashing lights that went off if the line had to be stopped for any reason. The flashing lights spurred the manufacturing engineers to scramble down to join the mechanics, not only to figure out how to get the line moving again but also to devise "fixes" that would prevent further stoppage in the future.

Timely coordination among the internal functional units and external suppliers required for a continuous moving assembly line was largely enabled by modern IT. This work, in effect, represented the early evolution of managing by wire for Boeing and its extended virtually integrated organization.

NOTES

1. Condit/Nolan Skype interview on January 21, 2010.
2. Haeckel, Stephan H., and Nolan, Richard L., "Managing by Wire," *Harvard Business Review* (September–October 1993), 122–132.
3. Mrs. Fields Cookies was founded in 1977 by Debbi Fields and her husband, Randy, and the brand is still active today.
4. Haeckel and Nolan, "Managing by Wire," *HBR*, p. 124.
5. We use this analogy in our HBR article: "Managing by Wire," *op cit.*
6. In the retail environment, the Zara Corporation has extended the concepts pioneered by Debbi and Randy Fields. See the Zara IT case slides: www.slideshare.net/raulpin101/zara-it-case, accessed by author on December 27, 2013.
7. Google has incorporated advanced techniques of AI (Artificial Intelligence) into its search engine software, which enables data mining of millions of searches from Google users and applies "learning" heuristics for continuous culling of more effective and efficient searches.
8. For a discussion of the evolution of ADP and EDP (Electronic Data Processing) into modern twenty-first-century information-processing giants, see Alfred Chandler and James Cortada (eds), *A Nation Transformed by Information* (Oxford University Press, 2003). Also, in chapter 7 of that book, "Information Technology Since 1960," the author relates the overall development of computing as it evolved in the Boeing Corporation.
9. See www.olive-drab.com/od_other_military_industrial.php3, accessed by author on July 7, 2011, and the Boeing Company website at: www.boeing.com/history/boeing/b17.html, accessed by author on January 3, 2011.
10. George Schairer exercised his multiple talents during a memorable weekend when a group of Boeing engineers responded to a request by the Wright Patterson Air Force group to switch out turbo-prop engines with ram-jet engines on a bomber airplane proposal—the B-52. The team did this with Schairer's artist rendition and fully painted model displaying the new airplane to the Wright Patterson group at the start of the next week. See: www.nytimes.com/2004/12/14/obituaries/14schairer.html.
11. The process of fully automating manufacturing parts and finished products from drawings to physical objects is rapidly advancing through innovations in 3-D printers equipped with raw material feeders, which offer the promise of increased speed and lower costs.
12. Vogt, Bill V., and Hall, Robert W. "Doc," "Part 1: "What You Can Do When You Have To," *Target: Innovation at Work*, 15, no. 1, (1999). In the 1930s and 1940s, household brushes and cleaners were sold by an army of Fuller Brush Company salesmen who went door to door making house calls and deliveries. These salesmen became famous for having just what the housewife needed, which the salesmen generally had in his car or truck, but if not, he would deliver the item in a timely manner.
13. West, H. Oliver, "What Is the Multiline System?" *Boeing News*, 1943.
14. From Boeing Company, Image B1219506: "737 Assembly Lines in Renton, circa 1982."

15. From Boeing Company, Image B1214566: "737 Net Generation Moving Line Manufacturing." Also. further described in Austin, R. D, Nolan, R. L., and O'Donnell, S., HBS Case #9–607–130, "The Boeing Company, Moonshine Case with Moonshine Improvements Highlighted," Exhibit 2 "The 737 Moving Line," April 3, 2007, p. 18.

BIBLIOGRAPHY

Austin, Robert D, Nolan, Richard L., and O'Donnell, Shannon, "The Boeing Company, Moonshine Case," Harvard Business School Case #9–607–130, April 3, 2007.

Haeckel, Stephan H., and Nolan, Richard L., "Managing by Wire," *Harvard Business Review* (September–October 1993), 122–132.

Vogt, Bill V., and Hall, Robert W. "Doc," "Part 1: "What You Can Do When You Have To," *Target: Innovation at Work*, 15, no. 1 (First Quarter 1999).

West, H. Oliver, "What Is the Multiline System?" *Boeing News*, 1943.

6 From Vertical to Virtual Integration

The advent of standardization between vertically integrated layers changes industry structure, as illustrated by the competition between IBM and Microsoft during the 1990s. As shown in Figure 6.1, both IBM and the computer industry were vertically integrated. IBM designed and manufactured the semiconductor chip for their computers' CPUs, fabricated the parts into an assembled computer system, and provided the computer operating system, as well as software applications, sales, and service. IBM also had the major market share for mainframe computers, minicomputers, and personal computers.

IBM senior management was aware of the growing market for personal computers and had responded by bringing out their own branded personal computer, the highly successful IBM PC. However, in introducing the PC, IBM concluded that its vertically integrated organization structure and its associated cost structure was too high to produce a competitively priced PC that could compete with Apple's PC—and it was.

As a result, the senior management decided to depart from the strategy that required a vertically integrated structure for in-house design and manufacture of IBM computers. The revised strategy called for outsourcing major components of the PC to a group of newly established IBM partners. The CPU of the IBM Personal Computer would be outsourced to Intel, the operating system to Microsoft, applications to WordStar (word processing), Lotus (spreadsheet), and sales to independent retailers including Sears.

The implementation of this strategy required IBM to disclose the interfaces between the vertical layers to their new external partners, as illustrated in Figure 6.2.

Figure 6.2 also shows the unintended result of this decision. Once the standard interfaces were disclosed and adopted by the outsourcing partners, IBM was forced to adhere to those interfaces rather than change them at will in response to competitors, as IBM had done in the past.[1] Once standard interfaces were disclosed outside IBM, a flurry of new entrants fiercely competed at each level of the vertical layers, resulting in the horizontalization of

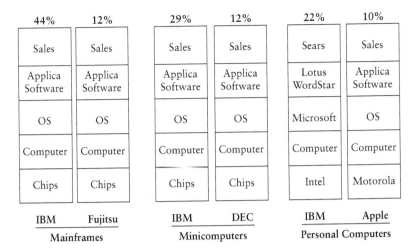

Figure 6.1 Vertical Computer Industry Structure 1991 and IBM's Segment Market Shares

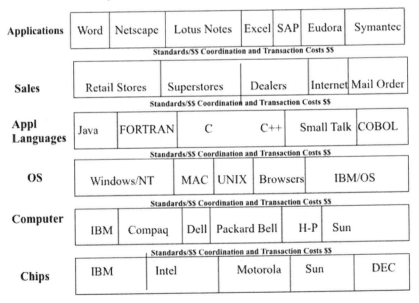

Figure 6.2 The New Horizontal Computer Industry Structure

the computer industry structure with multiple competitors at each level. The new level of competition increased the pace of innovation and accelerated price competition.

Microsoft focused on the intermediate level of PC operating systems and went on to dominate the industry segment, and in doing so achieved a higher corporate market value than IBM. IBM retained its vertically integrated cost structure and eventually experienced crippling financial losses. With no end to losses in sight, IBM's board hired an outside CEO to transform the company in a manner that the incumbent CEO did not accomplish.

The outside CEO, Lou Gerstner, and his executive team led the transformation of the IBM Corporation into a virtually integrated structure, but focused on the highest level of the value chain—that is, the service layer. IBM consulting services assisted companies with IT systems integration and eventually accounted for more than half of IBM's revenue.

Similar forces created the high-cost crisis for Boeing's commercial airplane business when Airbus introduced price competition that Boeing could not match with its vertically integrated structure and twentieth-century factories. Boeing eventually transformed its manufacturing operations to continuous moving line assembly, but the restructuring required a lot of change and learning.

Like IBM, Boeing struggled while learning how to manage the standard interfaces among the dynamically changing modules of the 787 as the airplane evolved from design to manufacturing. Lacking a process for smooth but intense and continued collaboration among the unprecedentedly large roster of parts and subassembly module outsourcers for the 787, confusion and delays rose to epidemic levels in the overall supply chain.

The Boeing Corporation still suffers from retaining much of its highly decentralized structure roughly depicted in Figure 6.3.

The essential elements of the Boeing formal organization are levels: headquarters, businesses, products, and lower-level functions. Important other dimensions, not illustrated in Figure 6.3, run across the hierarchical structure to facilitate its working. These include line/staff delineations, shared matrix responsibilities, and a large supply chain network of external outsourcers.

While Boeing is one of the largest users of IT, its current organization structure reflects a critical missing element: the strategic use of IT to support a more efficient streamlined global network and turn it into a competitive advantage. The gap becomes apparent by comparing IBM's IT-enabled organization and its key role in transforming the IBM organization structure with IT's lesser position in Boeing's organizational structure. Under Gerstner's leadership, IBM's CIO structure was consolidated from more than one hundred decentralized CIOs to a more streamlined and coordinated structure with a clearly designated CIO executive responsible for strategic leadership.

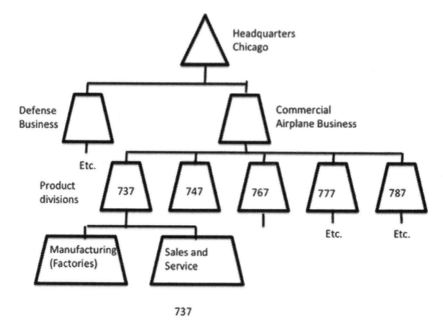

Figure 6.3 Boeing's Prevailing Hierarchical Organizational Structure

Both companies were industry leaders. Both encountered a competitive crisis brought on by high costs relative to emerging competitors less encumbered by the costs of decentralized vertical integration. More active innovation and price competition among industry layers eventually flowed through to the price and performance of the product. The result was price competition that the incumbent industry leader had difficulty in responding to in a timely manner—partially because of difficult organizational structure changes required to achieve a more efficient cost structure.

Like Boeing, IBM was vertically integrated but was on the road to cope with the inefficiencies, as evidenced by its strategy for introducing its highly successful PC computer. But IBM's traditional vertically integrated structure and company culture lingered, along with its noncompetitive high cost problems. IBM's crisis was unexpected and resulted in several years of multibillion-dollar losses. The incumbent CEO's incremental actions proved ineffective, and the problem was not resolved until the board went outside for CEO leadership.

In the Boeing situation, the outside competition was more direct and obvious, and the CEO leadership was in the process of executing a broad strategy for retention of industry leadership into the twenty-first century but with little sense of urgency. When Airbus took over industry leadership at the turn of the century, Boeing accelerated the execution of the 2016 strategy, including implementing the 737 moving line to stem the loss of market share on their "bread-and-butter" 737 airplane, and extensive outsourcing in their 787 program.

In contrast to Boeing, IBM was caught in a crisis of crippling financial losses. The new IBM CEO approached transformation with urgency and a total corporate structure perspective. He brought in an experienced CFO from a company that had been transformed.

The new IBM CFO launched a program to directly address IBM's cost structure problem. He broadly benchmarked business processes costs across the entire corporation, such as cost of hiring an employee, paying an invoice, carrying inventory, and manufacturing. The benchmarking went across industries and sought to determine "best in class." Best in class costs were compared to IBM's costs and became the new set of goals for developing a competitive IBM cost structure.

Upon doing the analysis of best in class business processes, IBM discovered that almost invariably IT enabled both greater efficiency and innovative ways of carrying out business processes. In addition, IBM discovered that in many cases, outsourcing through virtual vertical integration with strategic partners was preferable to in-house vertical integration. Indeed, Boeing discovered this too with the design and manufacture of the 787. But without raising the role of IT to the level of a strategic advantage, execution problems plagued the 787 program. The concept of using such a revolutionary global airplane as a springboard for product-driven transformation of the whole company eventually fell by the wayside.

The IBM CEO leadership team adopted a strategic approach to IT as they transformed their organization from multiple decentralized business processes to corporate-wide standardization on central, shared business processes. The Boeing CEO leadership team did not do this, essentially running its existing businesses as before, and localizing innovation and restructuring to each new product program. When the 787 program ran into difficulty, the tendency in crisis mode was to bail it out and revert to old processes— a reaction that was no longer viable for a program that was meant to be transformative.

BUILDING AN IT-ENABLED NETWORK ORGANIZATION

So in the big picture, IBM transformed more toward an IT-enabled networked organization. The centralized IT-enabled core business processes such as accounting, order entry, human resources (payroll and benefits and career management) and supply chain provided the backbone for a virtually integrated organization suitable for twenty-first-century operations.

Before IBM's transformation, its decentralized organization structure and systems were redundant and often resulted in customers being called on by different IBM teams with redundant and confusing product lines.

These decentralized IBM units were uncoordinated in providing one IBM face to the customer, and the customer often was confused by uncoordinated service such as receiving multiple bills from IBM, further confusing both the customer and IBM on what overall business IBM was doing with its customers.

The strategy enabled IBM to secure an efficient and competitive cost structure, and an efficient capability to embrace customers' total IT systems needs by providing a coordinated capability in systems integration to create collaborative strategic partnerships with a dynamic set of global partners.

Another important difference between IBM and Boeing had to do with their strategic acquisitions. IBM had created its strategic IT architecture and then made its strategic acquisition of the Price Waterhouse consulting business unit. Accordingly, IBM had a strategic core IT architecture to organizationally integrate the Price Waterhouse Consulting Unit. IBM's vertical integration by doing everything in-house was changed to creating a network of strategic partners to create a virtually integrated extended organization to service its customers.

Boeing had not developed an integrated IT strategic architecture. So Boeing sort of glued on the McDonnell-Douglas business units without an integrated IT architecture in place. The result was that the McDonnell-Douglas business units ran pretty much as they did before the merger, and those that were combined with Boeing were left to their own means for integration. Of course, there was a lot of corporate-speak rhetoric of being "one company" under the surviving Boeing corporate name on the buildings and letterhead, but the underpinning architecture was critically missing.

Boeing had been on a path of creative destruction of its twentieth-century organization structure and creative construction toward an IT-enabled virtually integrated network structure, but progress slowed to a crawl with 787 execution problems as well as by a cumbersome overly decentralized twentieth-century organization structure.

Further, while Boeing continues to be a leading user of IT, IT leadership is everywhere in Boeing, but strategic IT leadership (such as that at IBM) was diffused to the point that in reality, it was nowhere. The strategic vision and leadership from the top went missing for IT at Boeing.

MANAGING BY WIRE AND CEO LEADERSHIP

Even though Condit's CEO successors formally retained Condit's 2016 strategy for Boeing, they failed to embrace the enabling role of IT by providing strategic IT leadership. Consequently, instead of a coordinated corporate-wide transformation similar to CEO Lou Gerstner's approach for IBM, specifying "do it this way," Boeing worked with its existing decentralized functional hierarchies, empowering employees to "do it the best way you know how."

The transformations of many successful twentieth-century corporations are plagued with a similar condition—that is, they don't start with redesigning their corporate structures to an IT-enabled network organization structure that removes the inherent redundancies of their legacy decentralized divisional/functional structures. They further fail to incorporate the integral man/computer concepts whereby humans and computer architecture work together in a whole greater than the sum of its parts.

FROM "MAKE AND SELL" TO IT-ENABLED "SENSE AND RESPOND"

A fundamental requirement for moving between old and new corporate realties is overcoming technological constraints to the key strategic shift from "make and sell" to "sense and respond."

It is painfully obvious that no corporation can transform itself overnight. Every corporation has a capacity to change based upon its leadership and people. Transformation is the simultaneous combination of creative destruction and creative construction, governed by the capacity and will of the people in the corporation to change. Transformation requires a shared company-wide vision of a desired end state goal, a good strategy to get to the goal, and the persistent execution over time of actions toward the goal.

The Make-and-Sell Organization

In twentieth-century "make-and-sell" functional hierarchies, the pace of execution was based upon two widely used management tools: the accounting chart for resource allocation, and the organization chart showing the chain of command and the related hierarchical paths of communication. Each box on the organization chart cross-referenced to a number from the accounting chart, showing who had responsibility for the specific cost and revenue expectations for each part of the company.

The chart of accounts defined resources in financial terms. Annual budgeting started with an expression of the products and services to be produced during the year and what resources would be required by each "box" to do their part of the work required to create the product or service. Further identification was made between line boxes—those that directly created the product—and staff boxes (or overhead boxes)—those that provided services required for production activities such as executive management, inventory purchasing, and accounting services.

Once a budget was compiled including annual revenue and expenses, management control and accountability were exercised by monitoring monthly, quarterly, and annually the performance of each "box" and level on the organization chart in meeting their production and financial budgets. Communication of budget performance went from the lowest level of the organization up through the levels with increased summarization at each level all the way to the top of the organization whereby it could be determined whether or not revenues and expenses were "on budget" for a point in time of the year. This process was known as budget variance analysis, and the leader of each box was held accountable for meeting the relevant budget during the execution process.

The accounting model served to help manage the business toward achieving its goals. Managers throughout the chain of command grew so accustomed to staying on budgetary targets that "a good manager can manage anything" became the established wisdom of the era.

The annual budget served as the heartbeat of the corporation, and as the budgetary processes continued to be refined, budget variance analysis and reactions quickened to quarterly budgets and then monthly budgets. These increasingly shorter periods enabled more timely and efficient adjustments to resource allocation. However, the up-and-down chain of command communication architecture was hardwired into the functional hierarchy organization structure. Maintaining chain of command communications was important to the orderly coordination of corrective action involving the thousands of activities and thousands of workers in the large mass production operations of the twentieth century. Because of the difficulty of altering annual revenue and expense budgets during the year, the overall budgetary process of the twentieth-century corporations became characterized as "make and sell"—that is, a corporation plans on what to make during a year, makes it, and sells it. The desire for a controlled process generally trumps any opportunity to make in-course adjustments to unexpected developments.

The Sense-and-Respond Organizations

However, increasingly sophisticated IT continued to enable more efficient processes leading to quarterly budgets, then monthly budgets, and then with the advent of real-time network era technologies during the late twentieth century, several leading financial institutions began closing their accounting books daily for their operations around the world.

It was understandable that a new way of operating could emerge from financial institutions, which used computers to move intangible monetary resources around the world as electronic pulses and were thus able to sense and respond to their customers' needs in real time. Next in line to take IT-enabled "sense and respond" into the physical realm of products was the relatively young computer industry, with Cisco Systems leading the way.[2] Cisco Systems redefined their corporate structure as an "extended organization," including their global outsourcing supply chain partners and customers around the world. Cisco then went onto streamline its hierarchical organization structure by creating a shadow network of partners and customers connected through its IT-enabled network. Throughout the extended

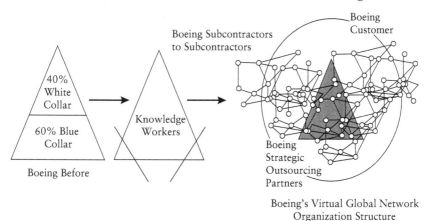

Figure 6.4   Creative Destruction/Construction from Boeing's Decentralized Hierarchical Organization toward an IT-Enabled Network Organization

organization, real-time information allowed everyone—Cisco management as well as partners and customers—to monitor the supply chain, manufacturing, customer orders, and order fulfillment.

Although not using the term "sense and respond," Boeing's 787 program was indeed intended to spearhead Boeing's transformation into a twenty-first-century sense-and-respond corporation.[3] The vision was to build the 787 organization from a clean sheet of paper, or as often described: building a "greenfield" organization. Because the process of change is essentially one of creative destruction, the overall organization would morph into a hybrid with an extended IT-enabled network structure floating over elements of a functional hierarchical organization structure as shown in Figure 6.4.

DESIGNING AND IMPLEMENTING THE INTELLIGENT CORPORATION

It wasn't so much a flawed vision or a poor strategy that caused Boeing's troubles with its 787 program; it had more to do with the lack of top management involvement and leadership in putting the pieces together into a coherent whole and executing. In contrast to the Cisco CEO's involvement in designing and daily use of its integrated managing by wire extended organizational system, neither of Phil Condit's successors as CEO was similarly involved—they seemed to fly too high over the detail, so to speak. Amalgamated, nonintegrated company cultures led to confusion on what to do and how to do it; nonintegrated and rationalized IT core systems for supply chain management led to inefficient and uncoordinated activity among organizational units and workers and a continuous stream of work delays;

intervention by a disengaged executive management team along with firings only made matters worse.

THE THREE CRITICAL ELEMENTS
OF MANAGING BY WIRE

There are three critical elements of a managing by wire IT infrastructure: connecting, sharing, and structuring information.

Connecting is the extent to which the IT infrastructure links information sources including media, location, and users. Many companies today are crisscrossed with independent networks and legacy systems that are technically incompatible and remain unconnected.

Boeing's PLM (Product Lifecycle Management) system connected Boeing engineers and managers during the 787 design phase, but it did not go deep enough into its extended organization supply chain beyond the thirty Tier 1 partners—for example, to detect the fastener hoarding during manufacturing that led to the first formally announced delivery delay of the 787.

Sharing information in the extended network organization taps into the collective intelligence and creativity potential of collaborative work. Getting everyone on the same page in a large corporation requires a capability not only to share information but also to share interpretations of the information and determine the appropriate response to be executed by business processes—both by wire and by people. For example, the excessive advanced purchase of fasteners by corporations in the Boeing 787 supply chain was not detected in a timely manner because of the IT infrastructure that did not connect suppliers or provide timely information to be interpreted as hoarding, causing widespread shortages during manufacturing.

Structuring information involves developing information *about* information—such as how information is classified, organized, and used.[4] It provides the basis for sharing and a common vocabulary for meaningful discussion and research. While the 787 manufacturing problem was eventually traced to fastener hoarding before corrective action was taken to resolve the problem, an appropriate managing by wire IT-enabled organization would have preempted the problem by detecting information about the anomaly, sharing it, and structuring it for appropriate action before it reached the crisis stage.

But the potential competitive advantages of managing by wire will most likely make the difference between corporations that survive and prosper in the twenty-first century and those that don't. The first major step toward effective use of IT technology for twenty-first-century corporations is mobilizing strategic IT leadership from the top. This top management leadership should include:

- a manage by wire enterprise model expressed in a common business language—not in IT terminology.

- determination of the scope of the extended networked IT-enabled organization.
- careful planning and monitoring of the pace of implementation at the senior most levels of the organization.

Extending the boundaries of the organization structure is difficult in respect to integration and establishing and maintaining relationships with strategic partners. The extended organization also must be built to support a sense-and-respond strategy. Thus, senior management must carefully decide which business units, if coordinated, would provide more value than the sum of their individual parts. For example, in the publishing industry, McGraw-Hill's strategy was to share their information systems and certain editorial content among multiple units. In contrast, Dun and Bradstreet kept their information systems and editorial content within the separate business units. McGraw-Hill shared information assets at the enterprise level, while Dun and Bradstreet shared their information assets only at the business unit level.

To be successful, Boeing's 787 new airplane program would have to share information assets with its strategic global partners. Indeed, Boeing's newly developed PLM system did this at the airplane design level, but fell short at the manufacturing level. Further, there was a lack of leadership in designing the interfaces of extended organization to provide a much broader business perspective than airplane design. Boeing's leaders seemingly assumed that the need for management control and coordination with partners building complete Tier 1 major components would be similar to the twentieth-century requirements for contractual outsourcing of parts—their critical continuous organizational learning thereby stagnated. And, as stated earlier, without an effective management by wire organization for tracking partners' activities down to the supply chain and the shop floor, Boeing's top management only discovered the critical disconnects when the first Boeing Dreamlifter delivered the first load of 787 components to the final assembly factory.

Boeing never embarked on an explicit and comprehensive strategy for managing by wire for the 787 airplane program, so there never was a comprehensive plan for its mission-critical implementation. Boeing's leaders were applying IT and capabilities toward a network structure, but an overarching and detailed vision of how the IT network would support the unprecedented complexity of outsourcing Tier 1 components to multiple strategic partners was lacking. As a result, there appeared to be frequent confusion between Boeing and its strategic partners in manufacturing and supply chain management. Ultimately, accountability for this omission and its impact must rest squarely with the CEOs and the Boeing board of directors.

Strategic IT leadership and results can only begin at the very top with the CEO and executive management team. The process must be constantly monitored by board-level oversight with board members who bring strategic IT savvy to the task.

NOTES

1. IBM's vertical integration between the layers of what might be thought of as Tier 1 systems had been maintained as proprietary IBM information. Competitors claimed that IBM had altered the standard interfaces between layers and retained the detail of the interfaces as proprietary information. Competitors whose products would not work in IBM computer systems such as disk storage, complained that IBM was engaging in a manner to constrain competition, which in turn led to federal antitrust action against IBM.
2. Austin, Robert D., Nolan, Richard L., and Cotteleer, Mark J., "Cisco Systems, Inc.: Implementing ERP." Harvard Business School Case 699–022.
3. I had conversations with Phil Condit about my concept of "sense and respond" before accepting the Philip M. Condit Endowed Chair at the University of Washington Foster School and after joining the UW faculty. We had a fairly congruent understanding of the potential role of network era IT in respect to transforming corporations from "make-and-sell" strategies to "sense-and-respond" strategies.
4. In science, the development of emerging bodies of knowledge begins with developing a taxonomy of relevant elements to enable people to discuss and research the elements toward theories. This process is evident in the study of plants, physics, and social sciences. In the emerging body of knowledge of IT management, my stage hypothesis of computer growth in corporations was based upon a taxonomy of growth process elements as reported in Nolan, "Managing Computer Growth: A Stages Hypothesis," *Communications of the ACM*, 16, no. 7 (1973), 399–405.

BIBLIOGRAPHY

Austin, Robert D., Nolan, Richard L., and Cotteleer, Mark J., "Cisco Systems, Inc.: Implementing ERP." Harvard Business School Case #699–022. Revised May 6, 2002.

Chandler, Alfred and Cortada, James (eds), *A Nation Transformed by Information* (Oxford, UK: Oxford University Press, 2003).

Haeckel, Stephan H., and Nolan, Richard L., "Managing by Wire," *Harvard Business Review* (September–October 1993), 122–132.

7   Managing Sustained Innovation

One of the most important and most difficult challenges for successful twentieth-century corporations in becoming successful twenty-first-century corporations is changing legacy structures built for managing innovation as a punctuated episodic phenomenon to new forms better suited to continuously sustained innovation. As we have discussed, twentieth-century corporations mostly grew to be very large through mass production. During this period, the balance of power between stewards (i.e., managers) and creators (R&D scientists, innovators) was—by design—heavily weighted toward stewards. One structural factor perpetuating the imbalance was separation in place of work and physical design. Management generally had offices in the factory complex. In contrast to factories and corporate headquarters, the places where creators worked looked similar to college campuses. Differences also included informality in dress, relationships, and appearance; and creators often sported beards and mustaches. Terms like "wild ducks," and at Boeing, "squirrels" were often coined to further maintain differentiation from stewards and became part of the company cultures of twentieth-century corporations.

Corporations like IBM, DuPont, and Xerox separated creators in "labs" that were generally geographically distanced from factories and corporate headquarters. IBM, headquartered in Armonk, New York, located its Watson Research labs in York Town Heights, New York, and Cambridge, Massachusetts, close to MIT-based collaborators. Xerox, headquartered in Rochester, New York, established its Xerox Parc lab in Silicon Valley close to Stanford University. Labs and research facilities closer to universities found it easier to hire and manage PhDs at these locations, and the locations facilitated collaboration with the research professors at the nearby academic institutions.

The annual planning ritual of these corporations typically had senior management stewards traveling to the labs. For example, at IBM senior management teams would travel to the labs to review research on new products and improvements for existing products. It was an outward-bound experience of sorts.

These meetings would typically go on for several days with creators formally presenting to the stewards. Inherent to the stewards' attitudes toward risk was considerable bias toward incremental product improvements, rather than breakthrough product developments. The stewards would caucus to decide what new products and product improvements they would introduce and manufacture for the coming year and what research programs they would resource for future years.

The meetings were crucial for the creators since the decisions largely dictated their work for the coming year. As a result, the meetings were often plagued by heated discussion and conflicts between stewards and creators. The stewards tended to have the last say on resource decisions, and severe disagreements sometimes resulted in the departure of talented creators. Some of the creators would decide not to seek employment at another corporation, and would start their own companies built around their ideas and inventions. A number of these start-ups became highly successful enterprises from which the original corporation could have benefitted by finding ways to keep the creator and the research in-house.

Another flash point of contention between the creators and stewards came from the oppressive employment contracts that often overreached in attempting to use legal means to ensure that ideas developed by creators while employed by the corporation became corporate property. Exit interviews were used to remind the creators of the noncompete clauses in their employment contracts and to warn that the corporation would use the full force of the law to enforce them.[1]

REUNITING ENGINEERS AND FACTORY WORKERS FOR CONTINUOUS SUSTAINED INNOVATION

As twentieth-century corporations mastered the practice of mass production, innovation emerged as the most promising way to achieve competitive advantage. The physical separation of creators from factory locations began to seem artificial, cumbersome, and detrimental to innovation in manufacturing methods and product development. Looser and more informal approaches toward scientists and innovators at successful corporations like 3M became important tools for keeping the creators and their ideas within the company.

At Boeing, the move toward Japanese-inspired lean manufacturing led to the innovative redesign of factories and moving assembly lines, with the workspaces of production engineers located above the factory floor with windows overlooking the moving line. These workspaces had direct line of sight to colored lights indicating the status of the moving line. Lights turned red and alarms went off when trouble caused the moving line to stop. A stopped line would send production engineers scurrying down to the line to collaborate with factory workers, diagnose the problem, and share ideas to get the line moving. This kind of multidisciplined collaboration led to innovation in methods for permanent line improvements—and sustained innovations in manufacturing efficiency emerged as a new competitive weapon.

This new environment facilitated more rapid innovation in product manufacturing and, often, redesign of the product itself to accommodate more efficient manufacturing. It also induced greater communication and collaboration between stewards and creators. As large corporations learned more about the process, the multidisciplinary approach soon led to more advanced forms of sustained innovation, involving multiple organizations over extended time periods.

LESSONS FROM THE CREATION OF THE INTERNET

Slowly but relentlessly, the impact of ever-improving IT was changing the character of innovation. Virtual integration and electronic communications transformed the creative work from geographically localized activities within individual corporations to broad collaboration among multiple, far-flung contributing entities. But it took a long time for most corporations to understand the potential of the Internet beyond increasing management efficiency, for example, by moving from annual to quarterly budgeting, and from there to continuous dynamic real-time resource allocation.

Most of corporate America collectively discovered the Internet in 1995 with Netscape's commercialization of the browser—the last piece needed to fully commercialize the Internet. Within a few years, seemingly overnight, literally every major corporation and business was on the Internet with its own website. In 2005, CNN listed the Internet as the number one non-medical invention since 1980, according to a panel of technology leaders assembled by the Lemelson-MIT Program.[2]

Beginning in the mid-1990s, my Harvard Business School colleague, Rob Austin, and I, along with our full-time research assistant, Erin Sullivan, launched a major research study on how the Internet was created and who created it.[3] We traced the vision of the Internet to an original article, "As We May Think," appearing in 1945 in the *Atlantic Monthly* and authored by Vannevar Bush.[4] Bush went onto become the President of MIT, where he pursued his vision and presided over the beginnings of the Internet as an ongoing collaborative effort among universities and government. That work led to the demonstration of the Internet, in 1969, for major corporations including IBM and AT&T.

When we talked to Internet pioneer Bob Taylor, who was present at the preview conferences for both IBM and AT&T, he reflected on the idea that "people think that the Internet happened overnight. They are wrong. It took forever." Taylor described IBM's reaction at the conference as, "Why would we be interested in the Internet? Our computers already 'talk to each other.'" He described the response at AT&T as loud "booing" by AT&T conference participants, who Taylor described as arrogantly seemingly to think that AT&T already owned the network industry.

As part of our research, we mapped the careers of over sixty Internet pioneers as they migrated through various organizations including universities, the federal government, corporations, and a new form of organization called Lincoln Labs from the 1960s into the 2000s. The migration reflected two factors. First, it was frequently triggered by a conflict with steward-like control structures imposed on the creators' work. Second, creators frequently moved to organizations that seemed to have communities of more like-minded creators.

Examples include Gene Amdahl leaving IBM and founding Amdahl Corporation in 1970 to develop IBM-compatible computers, but with an emphasis on open systems versus proprietary systems; and Bob Metcalfe leaving Xerox Parc to found 3Com in 1979, a computer network company based on Ethernet.

Steve Jobs, CEO of Apple, entered into a loose partnership with Xerox. Upon visiting Xerox Parc, Jobs saw the results of the creators' developments of networked, graphically interfaced PCs. He noted: "Xerox doesn't realize what they've got." He hired away some of the Xerox creators, including Alan Kay, and developed and commercialized a breakthrough PC: the Apple Macintosh. Many similar examples account for the hundreds of billions of dollars of value created and captured from the ideas and innovations that arose with the development of the Internet.

A CONTRIBUTING PROBLEM: FLAWED INCENTIVE SYSTEMS

Stewards and creators in corporations have always realized that they need and must rely on each other. But one of the most common flash points for conflict comes from the inequities creators perceive in corporate legacy twentieth-century incentive systems intended to motivate creators in their work. It is instructive to review the common issues that come up when such conflicts arise and the dynamics of trying to resolve them.

One such discussion between the CEO of an aerospace company and his Vice President for Aeronautical Engineering and New Product Development illustrates the common issues and dynamics of the conflict.[5] After a prior meeting on another subject, the CEO asked the engineering executive how he might be of assistance to her and her engineering department. The engineering executive paused and then decided to open the can of worms that had been an ongoing problem for her. She responded tersely and more strongly than intended, "The bloody metric-based bonus system was killing creativity, motivation, and performance of my engineers."

This response surprised the CEO and was atypical coming from this executive. In timely follow up, the CEO called for a meeting including himself, an aeronautical engineer from the Vice President for Aeronautical Engineering and New Product Development organization to explain the dysfunction, and the HR executive who was responsible for the design and operation of the corporate incentive system.

The CEO opened the meeting by asking the aeronautical engineer to explain to the group assembled the problems with the merit pay system. He got right to the point: "The merit system doesn't work because it is based on a flawed idea."

The HR executive bristled: "Our merit pay system results from a two-year study done in collaboration with one of the very best HR consulting firms in the world. We examine how it's working and refine it every year, in collaboration with those same external, international experts."

In response, the engineer stood up and carefully and deliberately drew on the conference room whiteboard a picture with two axes, the vertical "y" axis labeled "value" and the horizontal "x" axis labeled "time." He drew two curves, one rising steadily, the other first rising, and then severely turning down to dip even below the horizontal axis. The first curve he labeled, "Merit pay system value." The second, down-turning one, he labeled, "Actual value."

He explained, "This picture tells a story that's at least partly implicated in just about every organizational and economic catastrophe you can think of: the Internet bubble, the mortgage crisis, the U.S. defense department overruns. You name it. All are situations in which we maximize something that we think is value, but it eventually turns out to be driving away from real value. Part of the problem is that over time people figure out how their performance is being evaluated and drive up that performance artificially. They 'game' the system.

"You executives *want* to incentivize us to create more value, but in fact you only really incentivize what you measure. You ask us to set quantitative goals, milestones to stretch for. You *say* you take into account some immeasurable factors. But in reality the most tangible evidence of performance is deemed what you can *measure*. So even though you tell us that we will be evaluated on a broad range of considerations, those measurable, quantitative performance measures—how many patents, that sort of thing—hang out there in space like glowing neon signs. Because those you know you can verify and defend when you are confronted with our perceived unfairness in the process. The immeasurable, intangible stuff is a lot more ambiguous and harder for you to evaluate.

"If I'm an unscrupulous R&D guy, and I know you've got a bias toward what you can measure, or that anyway you think those are the clearest indicators of my performance, I might just start to slide down my effort toward the measurable indicators. Since I'm moving away from the 'ideal,' I'm reducing the real value to the business to increase my measured performance indicators. And if I do have scruples, I'm unhappy because you're putting me in competition with this other R&D person who might just be unscrupulous enough to do whatever looks good. I might even feel that I must move away from the ideal, as much as I might not want to, in order to prevent my managers from evaluating me as a poor performer compared to that unscrupulous person."

The CEO asked, "What if you just allocated more effort: you simply worked harder?"

The engineer responded, "I, personally, would do that. I'd work harder rather than move away from the allocation of my effort that I knew delivered better value for the business. But I and others like me would be really annoyed that I'm having to work a lot harder, *just* so I can look equally as good as someone gaming the incentive system to garner the same financial and further promotion rewards.

"You want us to have good ideas, not just a lot of ideas: a really good patent, not just a lot of them. If we have one really good idea, that might be worth more than a whole lot of not-as-good ideas."

The CEO reflected, "If it's a really good idea, it ought to generate more profits. Its economic value ought to be obvious."

The engineer was not deflected. He persisted in criticizing the incentive system, turning to the issue of figuring out how to allocate credit for the idea across the different members of an R&D staff. "Innovation is not an individual pursuit, not anymore. Most of the important work done in universities and corporations involves some type of collaboration, and at the end of the day it is difficult to tease apart who did what. On any given project, some contribute more than others. And even in a lot of projects, the contributions are not even. Managers' oversight of the work and insight into individual contributions is almost always less valid and reliable than those working on the projects. So the manager's decisions on individual rewards based on real contributions is always flawed to some extent. Discussions with individual workers and managers about personal merit rewards become unresolved exercises of frustration for both. This then tends to make merit systems dependent on measurable things that can be counted, combined, and made into numbers, or ratios, which further obfuscate understanding of merit pay plans."

At this point, the CEO had reached his limits of frustration and took control to shift the discussion to "good enough" merit incentive systems. He asked, "How do you know that we can't formulate measures that are 'good enough'? They might not be perfect, but they might be good enough."

The engineer cryptically and undiplomatically retorted, "That's a pipe dream. Many economists continue to write about this problem, but it hasn't changed practice. Managements continue to persist in *incentivizing* people to perform better because they're willing to assume that measures can be 'good enough.'"

"But it is a really shaky assumption—especially where innovative and collaborative work is involved. No such measures or measurement system magically spans all the dimensions essential to value creation. And in R&D,

innovators continue to rediscover and adjust what they do on a daily basis, as they learn from experiments, react to competition, and as new technologies make new things possible. So when managements, with insufficient understanding of innovation, design systems that try to influence how effort is allocated, they rarely, if ever, can get it right. In addition, there is the rather naïve associated problem that most merit pay systems are only adjusted once a year to correct for events that happen every day. If we are going to effectively tackle these real problems, management must dislodge themselves from overdependence on measurable metrics; instead, they must engage in the hard work of becoming more involved with what knowledge workers do, and build trust. To do so, managers would have to spend time with people, not just reports of performance. And managers would have to earn credibility with people, ensuring them that they wouldn't just fall back on easier-to-defend, less ambiguous quantitative measures."

It is about this time in these types of meetings, and often even before, when collective frustrations boil over. The VP of Human Resources in this case retorted, "Seems like the whole world is wrong because the whole world uses these systems. So what's the answer? Should we avoid quantitative measures altogether?"

The important lesson here is that the problem is not measurement; it's the idea of incentivizing by overreliance on rewards with quantitative measures, counts, and milestones. There is a big difference between looking into projects involving creative work in a serious, wide-ranging way and rewarding people based on what you find out, versus setting up some sort of precise counting scheme in advance that defines performance and associates it with compensation that people can game.

WHEN THE BALANCE BETWEEN STEWARDS AND CREATORS IS OFF

For eighty years of organic growth, Boeing benefitted from maintaining a delicate balance between its stewards and creators. Bill Boeing established the roots of the balance with the culture he fostered during the company's early years. This culture benefited from a tradition of promotion from within, which produced a healthy run of Boeing CEOs with aeronautical engineering backgrounds, who then equipped themselves and their potential successors with the formal business training necessary for effective collaborative work with the stewards of the company.

As Boeing surpassed $1 billion in annual revenues during the 1950s, the board broadened the pool of potential CEOs to those who did not necessarily have formal aeronautical engineering backgrounds but had substantial business training and experience at Boeing.

Simultaneously, Boeing formally recognized the importance and contributions of exceptional Boeing aeronautical engineers by designating their "legendary" organizational status and contributions as "Boeing Distinguished Engineers." These engineers included George Schairer, Joe Sutter, and others.[6] The legendary engineers were encouraged to wander through Boeing at will and engage in impromptu meetings and discussions with Boeing senior executives and engineers of major Boeing programs.[7]

This long-running delicate balance was shattered during the integration of the McDonnell-Douglas senior executive team into Boeing and the Boeing culture. The decisions at the time to further decentralize the Boeing organizational structure had the effect of balkanizing the Boeing and McDonnell-Douglas cultures, with the relocation of Boeing headquarters out of Seattle to Chicago and the infusion of McDonnell-Douglas executives with significant shareholder power into the board of directors. John McDonnell and Harry Stonecipher—the two largest shareholders of Boeing stock on the board—tipped the board toward a major emphasis on financial engineering. Things got worse with missteps by former McDonnell-Douglas executives (assigned to the new Boeing Defense division post-merger) in illegally hiring an Air Force contracts officer, resulting in the sudden resignation of Phil Condit, and the naming of Harry Stonecipher as Condit's CEO replacement. After a short run as CEO, Stonecipher had to be replaced, and the reconstituted Boeing board of directors chose a Boeing outsider with financial management experience similar to Stonecipher's over a Boeing insider—a legendary aeronautical engineer and CEO of the Boeing Commercial Airplane business unit. Almost like rolling thunder, it took just a few years to reach a tipping point that destroyed the delicate creator/steward balance at Boeing.

MAKING SUSTAINED INNOVATION WORK

As the economy has shifted from the twentieth century to the twenty-first century, the importance and sustainability of continuous innovation has dramatically increased. In our research,[8] we have identified a number of guidelines toward maintaining a healthy balance between stewards and creators.

Maintain the pool of creators as a valuable corporate asset, which it is. During the good times of the twentieth century, large successful corporations like IBM, DuPont, and many others maintained solid and consistent funding for R&D. Then during the harder times closing in on the twenty-first century, R&D expenditures were often among the first expenses/investments to be cut—viewed as a discretionary expense rather than a long-term asset. One year after Boeing's acquisition of McDonnell-Douglas, Boeing's R&D expenditures were dramatically cut including layoffs of R&D employees. The cuts were largely due to the shift in influence in top management by a new group of executive stewards focused on financial management. The result was to further delay a new commercial airplane program for more than a decade, allowing Airbus to rapidly close its new airplanes sales gap with Boeing.

It quickly became clear by the turn of the century, as Airbus continued to gain sales momentum, that R&D was not a discretionary expense, which could easily be cut and then increased at will. Further, twenty-first-century competition required sustained, not episodic innovation and nimble responses to emerging developments. This realization highlighted creators as an important Boeing corporate asset requiring continuous attention and management.

In fact, this lesson from Boeing applies to all corporations: the pool of corporate creators must be viewed and treated as a critical asset, and not a discretionary expense subject to cutting during difficult financial times. As an asset, the creator pool is built over long periods and effectively assimilated into a corporate culture over equally long periods. Further, it is an asset that cannot be quickly replaced once lost.

Maintain a balance in influence between stewards and creators. Stewards ultimately control and have the last say on the corporate purse strings. And stewards often don't see visions of the future as clearly as creators.[9] Sometimes it turns out that the stewards are right, and other times creators are proved right. But the power of the purse strings tends to swing the decisions more often toward stewards than creators. Consequently, many good creators can be easily lost in the process.

The lesson here is to listen to the arguments on each side with an open mind, maintain a long-term scorecard on actual outcomes, and strive to guard against the steward bias by better balancing decisions between stewards and creators. It is important to understand that new program decisions do not have to be fully funded at the outset but can be funded by a series of lesser amounts to keep a program alive while gaining more information for making an informed decision on its potential, risks and timing.

Build bridges between stewards and creators. Bridging communications between stewards and creators requires a special kind of professional. Distinguished Engineers at Boeing often served as effective bridges between stewards and creators.

These seasoned aeronautical engineers have built successful careers by innovating and then monitoring how their innovations become profitably commercialized over time. This background brings credible perspective and insights important to an effective decision process. It helps creators and stewards alike learn to nurture ideas and visions through the process of commercialization.

Some of Boeing's Distinguished Engineers went onto become CEO and/or served important roles on Boeing's board of directors. Their unique insights helped guide the oversight of Boeing's strategic program investments.

At Boeing there are many examples. George Schairer wandered into Phil Condit's office when Condit was the program manager for the Boeing 757. Schairer and Condit discussed the range for the 757, leading Condit to extend the range of the 757 to be able to fly across the United States nonstop from Seattle to Miami. Condit followed Shairer's advice, and today the Boeing 757 is still in active service because of its range capability. As a result, the Boeing 757 sustained a longer life than its direct competitor, the Airbus 320, which had a shorter range designed for the shorter air routes characteristic of Europe. On November 28, 2005, Boeing manufactured its last Boeing 757, ending a twenty-three-year manufacturing run. Only in January 2013 did Airbus reengineer its Airbus 320 to bring out the Airbus 321neo, at last providing a longer-range competitive replacement for the Boeing 757.

Joe Sutter, the legendary chief engineer of the 747, retained an office at Boeing's Commercial Airplane headquarters after retirement and actively "walked around" providing advice to the various Boeing commercial airplane programs including the Dreamliner.

Bob Taylor at Xerox Parc effectively bridged between stewards and creators. So did Bill Gates, who was able to understand and debate effectively as a peer with his talented software engineers, while maintaining a drive and sense for successfully commercializing innovations.

The lesson is that it is important to involve seasoned bridging professionals during debates and discussions that lead to decisions on investing in innovations.

Incorporate peer reviews during the cycle of innovations. Innovation is almost always a collaborative process among creators. Peer reviews among the collaborators often reveal important information about progress, timing, and resource requirements going forward. The lesson is that the peer review process should be integrated as a matter of course into the overall management of creating and commercializing innovations. And stewards need to invest the time and effort to understand the results and implications of the peer review. This means doing the work necessary to understand the base level vocabulary of the subject matter necessary to interact and ask the right questions for go/no-go investment decisions.

View innovation management as successive decisions to buy information that will inform a series of informed cost/benefit decisions over time. Creators work over time to take an idea, visualize what it can become, and then engage in a process of discovery to march the innovation toward a realized reality. Along the way, discovery unveils resources required, timing to reality, and potential returns. These three elements continuously require important go/no-go decisions to be made as the project develops. Effectively managing the innovation project can be likened to buying increasingly higher-quality information for making judgments and decisions—similar to the successive rounds of funding for new ventures.[10]

The lesson is that either a premature rush to closure, on the one hand, or a delay in making a go/no-go decision, on the other, represents a failure in management processes for the innovation project.

Conflict never completely goes away. The inherent differences in motivations of stewards and creators are value based and ones that will not completely go away. And since creators and stewards need each other in the corporate world, the severity of the conflict should not be left unchecked to fuel misunderstandings. So the lesson is to strive for mutual understanding of each other's positions and quality of thinking. Further, integrity and mutual trust among the parties is essential for effectively managing the innovation process.

NOTES

1. Over time as alleged violations of these contracts were litigated, the overreaching in these contracts was frequently unenforceable and viewed as a violation of the worker's rights.
2. See "Top 25 Innovations," June 19, 2005, http://as400blog.blogspot.com/2005/01/cnncom-top-25-innovations-jan-17-2005.html.
3. For a short description of our research, see "About the Research," Austin and Nolan, "Bridging the Gap between Stewards and Creators," *MIT Sloan Management Review* (Winter 2007), 30.
4. Bush, Vannevar, "As We May Think," *Atlantic Monthly*, 1 nos. 1&2 (January 1945), www.theatlantic.com/magazine/archive/1945/07/as-we-may-think/303881/ and note that I accessed it on September 15, 2014.
5. We fictionalized the meeting dialogue accounted for in this section, which also appeared in a similar form in our Harvard Business Press book: Austin, Robert, D., Nolan, Richard L., and O'Donnell, Shannon, *Harder Than I Thought* (Boston: Harvard Business School Press, 2013).
6. Joe Sutter was Chief Engineer of the Boeing 747, and upon retirement retained an office in Boeing's Commercial Airplane headquarters in Renton, Washington.
7. This practice of wandering around to facilitate knowledge sharing and collaborative work was also practiced by universities whereby deans paid particular attention to locating offices of professors in such a way that wandering around among professors in close proximity often led to collaborative work resulting in important academic research and academic publications. Harvard Business School Dean John MacArthur was especially skilled in influencing synergistic interactions that led to collaboration among business school professors that resulted in dynamics of improved classroom teaching and academic research. During my tenure on the Harvard Business School faculty, John's skill in this was often a topic of lunch discussions.
8. See Austin and Nolan, "Bridging the Gap Between Stewards and Creators," *Sloan Management Review*, 48, no. 2 (Winter 2007), 34–36.
9. This has been well researched and documented by Harvard Business School Professor Clay Christenson and reported in his book: *The Innovator's Dilemma* (Boston: Harvard Business Press, 1997).
10. Entrepreneurs often approach venture capitalists with grand ideas, arguing that their ideas will result in the next IBM, Google, or other successful enterprise, and that therefore the venture capitalist should invest, at the outset, the money necessary for the entrepreneurs to pursue their goals. The savvy venture capitalist generally nods and then steers the ambitious entrepreneurs toward the objective of first providing more evidence/information to validate their claim. And if the venture capitalist assesses the entrepreneur's idea with possible merit, he/she works with the entrepreneur in making a first-round modest investment to develop the idea more fully—in effect, the venture capitalist is buying further information to decide whether further rounds of investments are justified.

BIBLIOGRAPHY

Austin, Robert, and Nolan, Richard L., "Bridging the Gap between Stewards and Creators," *Sloan Management Review*, 48, no. 2 (Winter 2007), 29–36.

Austin, Robert D., Nolan, Richard L., and O'Donnell, Shannon, *Harder Than I Thought* (Boston: Harvard Business School Press, 2013).

Bush, Vannevar, "As We May Think," *Atlantic Monthly*, 1 nos. 1&2 (January 1945), 1–8.

Christenson, Clay. *The Innovator's Dilemma*. (Boston: Harvard University Press, 1997).

8 Managing Corporate Transformation

The backdrop for corporate transformation is the fundamental and relentless shift in the economic system. The last economic shift was the transition from the agrarian economy to the industrial economy that took place from the last half of the nineteenth century through the twentieth century, resulting in the growth of large corporations as we know them today. In chapter 2, "Then and Now," we highlighted the meaningful differences, for today's corporations between the industrial economy and the new economy. The new economy has been characterized using terms like "information," "knowledge," and "innovation." Almost all of these characterizations are based on advent of the digital computer and associated IT technologies, exploited by relatively new corporations like Amazon, Apple, and Zara.

From the perspective of economics and management theory, IT has given rise and prominence to information as a critical resource. As a resource, information differs from more familiar resources such as people, money, and materials. The information resource is not depleted when it is deployed; the generative value of the information resource increases with use. Further, the cost of the information resource continues to plummet as described in Moore's Law, which roughly has computing costs decreasing by half every eighteen months or so, while the volume and value of information explodes and becomes available to substitute for more costly resources. For example, IT and information have continued to be substituted for factory workers carrying out routine manual tasks, dramatically reducing the number of factory workers while increasing factory output and lowering costs. The substitution of one type of resource (e.g., IT-enabled robotics) for many others underlies the restructuring of major industries such as the automotive, financial service, and aerospace industries. This phenomenon parallels the way that energy resources were applied to mechanizing the farm, which dramatically reduced farm workers from 50 percent of the U.S. workforce at the beginning of the twentieth century to lower than 2 percent of the workforce today, even as output continues to increase. Today, with many fewer workers, U.S. agriculture remains the second biggest producer of crops and livestock in the world, just behind China.

And similar to the economic shift from the agrarian economy to the industrial economy, the shift from the industrial economy to the information economy has resulted in new value creation opportunities such as global outsourcing, new information-based products (smartphones, computer search engines, electronic book readers, social media) and real-time any time, any place communication services provided by relatively new corporations such as Facebook, Twitter, and LinkedIn. The structure and processes of corporations designed for the industrial economy are continually being transformed to those of the information economy.

Corporations that were founded at the dawn of the twenty-first century started in a mature information technology environment in the network era (1995–2015+). Earlier mainframe and microcomputer technologies had made IT ubiquitous in the twentieth-century corporations. But the new ones—like Amazon, Google, and Facebook—had the opportunity to start out with IT-enabled network structures rather than relying on the more limited IT that twentieth-century corporations had built to manage their more conventional decentralized hierarchies.

The IT network technologies not only impacted the organizational structures but were also extended into products, services, and extended partnerships with other corporations. Amazon and Google built their company cultures within an IT-rich environment that enables both internal and external connections and interactions to serve business needs as naturally as "the air we breathe."

In contrast, corporations such as Boeing, IBM, Otis Elevator, and even Cisco, that were founded and grew in the twentieth century (and earlier for Otis, established in 1853), needed to transform legacy systems from the old "make-and-sell" business environment to a significantly different "sense-and-respond" interactive relationship with their customers.

The shift from the industrial economy to the information economy differs from the earlier transformation, where agricultural workers took on factory jobs. As we discussed earlier, the current transition from industrial work to knowledge or information work requires high levels of sustained innovation in applying IT technologies to create value and a faster pace of change as improved ways of doing work are learned.

As in the previous economic transition, even though the nature of work changes, the values from the old economy linger with workers. Just as the agrarian ethos of "early to bed, early to rise," and the "early bird gets the worm" morphed into the eight-hour workday at a fixed location, today's new knowledge work has become more global, pervasive, and continuous rather than regimented into standard shifts.

THE RISE OF THE TWENTY-FIRST CENTURY CORPORATION

Successful models of twenty-first-century corporations continue to redefine the concepts of work, management, and collaboration. These models commonly include integration of strategic uses of IT, virtually integrated organizational networks with global partners in extended organization and supply chain systems, real-time dynamic allocation and management of resources, and sustained innovation. Becoming a successful twenty-first-century corporation entails understanding what is and isn't likely to succeed in the new economy, creating a vision for the twenty-first century and defining a strategy to enact the vision, and executing the creative destruction/creative construction management process necessary to achieve the strategy.

Corporations founded during the twenty-first century have grown up during a time when network technologies were relatively mature, commercialized, and available for use in building organization structures, integrating products and services, and working with customers and partners. For the corporations that recognized and seized this opportunity, there is no need to transform to a twenty-first century-corporation; they are already there.

To understand what a successful twenty-first-century corporation can be, it is informative to follow a success story built from the ground up—the now often told history of Amazon.com and its founder, early digital native[1] Jeff Bezos.

Born in 1962, Bezos graduated summa cum laude from Princeton University in computer science and electrical engineering. After graduation, he worked at D. E. Shaw, a specialized investment management firm focused on companies that exploited the economics of technological innovations. Bezos specialized in Internet technologies and developed a list of the top twenty potential opportunities for building new businesses. "Books" made the top of his list.

The business of books is where Bezos decided to gain a foothold for his venture. The business proposition can be simply stated: the cost of an inventory of books in a physical bookstore versus a virtual bookstore is dollars versus pennies. The same holds true for the cost (and time) of distributing books to customers from many physical bookstores versus one virtual bookstore. And it is even more cost effective if the physical book can be virtualized and distributed over the Internet to customers.

Over time, Bezos's vision extended beyond books to the retail industry itself. So the long-range plan was for Amazon to become the world's virtual retail corporation. Bezos started with books and leveraged the learnings out to other susceptible retail products and stores.

With modest resources, Bezos began the IT coding for his virtual bookstore as his wife started their car journey from the East Coast to Seattle—the place Bezos chose for his new venture. Bezos arrived in Seattle, rented a house, launched his virtual bookstore in the mythical garage, got orders, bought some books wholesale from Ingrams, and fulfilled the orders from his garage. Physical books were shipped to customers in the beginning; creating virtual books to ship over the Internet would come later.

Bezos chose Seattle to locate his venture for a number of reasons including that Ingrams, a major book distributer, was located in nearby Oregon. Bezos also chose Seattle because the Puget Sound region was a high-tech industry commons including Boeing, Microsoft, and the University of Washington—all of which contributed to a source of talented software engineers—the type of workers needed to build a virtual retail store and to virtualize products and services.

Bezos succeeded in books, creating a virtual Amazon bookstore, and then went on to create a virtual print technology that allowed books to be read comfortably on an electronic screen, Amazon's Kindle. Customers could use the Kindle to instantly buy, download, store, and read hundreds of books on a single device, substituting for doing the same by traveling to and from bookstores to buy hundreds of bulky physical books.

Bezos had a marketing flair too. He chose to name his venture "Amazon" to connote "huge"—the Amazon River has the largest flow of any river including the next largest, the Mississippi River. The then-industry leader, Barnes and Noble, brought legal action against Amazon for Amazon's claim of operating the "biggest bookstore in the world." The wide publicity of the legal action made Amazon instantly well known and further provided Bezos with a platform to educate the world on the realities of a virtual bookstore versus a "bricks-and-mortar" physical bookstore. Bezos's corporation changed the retail book industry, propelling it into the twenty-first century, and true to Bezos's vision, Amazon is pulling the rest of the retailing industry into the virtual world of the twenty-first century as well.

On the way, Bezos also challenged other twentieth-century conventions such as the management focus on short-term, annual planning, and evaluating corporate performance predominately by short-term metrics like annual EPS (earnings per share). Bezos's strategy was not to provide shareholders a steady stream of annual increases in EPS. Instead, Bezos embraced a "get big fast" strategy in order to gain a first-mover advantage in creating the virtual supermarket retail store. The strategy extended to investing in growth in other virtual retail stores. The process was fast paced: research the opportunity, experiment/prototype, decide—go/no-go; if go, scale it, and integrate it, to further Amazon's progress toward becoming the virtual retail industry supermarket leader. Similar to "search," Bezos was an early adopter of IT-enabled "rapid iteration" or experimentation with new ideas and innovations.

Through sustained innovation, Bezos has relentlessly leveraged the robustness of the IT-enabled architecture that he and his team created. By design, Amazon's platform for selling and distributing books has continued to morph to a platform for selling and distributing retail products and services in general. It has been guided by the idea of becoming the "Sears and Roebucks of the twenty-first century" through an increasingly clear vision of a "store to sell everything" and a steady track record of doing just that.

Bezos's strategy was out there for all to see (investors, employees, competitors and the public in general). Every year since the founding of Amazon, Bezos has republished his original strategy letter in Amazon's annual reports to its shareholders. He wanted to make sure that potential investors and employees of Amazon knew what they were getting into: what the overarching vision was, what the corporate strategy was, and how the strategy was going to be executed by the management team. Here again, Bezos challenged another characteristic of twentieth-century corporations—the predilection for secrets and proprietary information. Contrarily, Bezos advocated information transparency and wide communications. In a world of "Google it" and smartphones everywhere, events and happenings become known quickly and spread lightning fast. Unfortunately for many corporations, their executive teams and boards remain blinded by the lightning pace of twenty-first-century digital natives like Jeff Bezos.

Today, Amazon has succeeded in executing its strategy with revenues of more than $50 billion, and profits in the hundreds of millions. With approximately 50,000 employees, the Amazon workforce is generating about a million dollars per employee each year. Also true to his business philosophy, Bezos continues to invest heavily in long-term research and continued growth versus shorter-term profits.

Revenue per employee in greenfield twenty-first-century corporations like Amazon continues to overshadow that of twentieth-century corporate competitors attempting to transition to the new environment, such as Barnes and Noble ($200,000 in annual revenues per employee). Traditionally structured twentieth-century corporations have increased their revenue per employee as they have restructured their organizations and leveraged IT technologies. During the 1970s and into the 1980s, the average revenue per employee for large corporations ranged from under $100,000 to $150,000. IBM, for one, increased its revenue per employee from $150,000 during the 1990s to $230,000 by 2010. In the second decade of the twenty-first century, corporations continue to recover from the long and deep recession but are able to grow by maintaining their workforces at the current size, and continuing to leverage IT technologies.

Amazon exhibits another characteristic of successful twenty-first-century corporations as well: sustained innovation and commercialization of innovations. Amazon stays ahead of its competitors with innovative experiments and opportunistic scaling of both retail and wholesale-like products such as cloud computing for other corporations. Virtualization continues to serve up new competitive opportunities, but to discover the opportunities and shake down those that have commercialization potential requires being in the thick of learning what the opportunities are and the nature of exploiting them.

On a December 3, 2013, CBS TV broadcast of its flagship news program, *60 Minutes*, CEO Jeff Bezos unveiled and demonstrated a futuristic package delivery from an Amazon warehouse to a household by a small drone airplane. The next day critics decried a host of potential problems such as congested airspace, theft of packages dropped off at private homes, deliveries dropped on customers' heads, and many others. While some of these problems were described as showstoppers to commercialization, members of the Amazon culture were more likely to view them merely as part of an agenda to be addressed on the road to commercialization of an opportunistic innovation.

Google offers another example of a successful corporation founded in the twenty-first century, with annual revenue per employee exceeding $1 million. In contrast to Amazon's stated vision of virtualizing infrastructures and products in the retail industry, Google continued to mine its successful "search" services and embraced a broad innovation strategy of encouraging employees to spend one work day a week coming up with new ideas and innovations. This might be described as "letting a thousand flowers bloom"—and so far Google has been investing in many innovations.

With this approach, Google, in contrast to Amazon, applies a broader focus to innovation and commercialization. Consequently, there seems to be a less rigorous process for targeting Google innovations and less infrastructure to incorporate and scale promising innovations. Nevertheless, the Google culture remains welcoming and supportive to innovations and continues to produce promising ideas and products and services such as Google Maps, self-driving automobiles, and the Android smartphone operating system.

The vast majority of corporations that were founded and grew during the twentieth century have not enjoyed the opportunity of greenfield growth amidst the ubiquitous and maturing IT network technologies. These corporations scaled through mass production—or as we described it in chapter 1, Stage 2: Industrialization. Accordingly, those that have survived are faced with the difficult challenge of transforming their increasing obsolete forms to successful twenty-first-century forms.

FROM SUCCESSFUL TWENTIETH-CENTURY FORMS TO SUCCESSFUL TWENTY-FIRST-CENTURY ORGANIZATIONS

In part, the success of Amazon set off the dot-com boom, launching a myriad of twenty-first-century ventures and frenzy among twentieth-century corporation "wannabes." Corporations raced to establish Internet divisions and launched their own websites. But launching the corporate website was the easy part. To make a business of it, or to leverage the Internet into the corporation's traditional businesses, was much harder.

Americans in particular, seem quick to embrace new management fads but also quick to write them off. This is what happened during the dot-com boom. But contrary to popular opinion, following the inevitable "dot-bomb," the Internet was not overhyped, as we witness today. If anything the Internet was underhyped, and clearly not a sinking fad.

But most twentieth-century corporations got off on the wrong road by being fickle about the Internet opportunities and holding on too tightly and too long to obsolete organizational forms and management practices. As we learned, the road of transformation is long and difficult to travel. And there are many different routes that can lead to the destination.

Boeing had experienced a detour in executing its twenty-year vision and strategy to transform to a large systems integrator aerospace industry leader by 2016. Nevertheless, Boeing continues to make progress. By 2013, with $86 billion in revenue and a workforce of 169,000, Boeing's revenue per employee was about $510,000—a significant increase from its revenues per employee in the last half of the twentieth century, even though the company was at the forefront of exploiting IT technologies during the mainframe era (1960–1980) and the microcomputer era (1980–1995).

I went to work at Boeing in 1966, in the mid-mainframe era, as a systems simulation engineer in the Minuteman Program located in Boeing's Aerospace Division. I began my Boeing employment by being sent to Boeing's computer school full time for three months to learn Boeing's computers and polish my programming skills. During this time, Boeing was a leading computer user in automating business systems such as payroll and inventory control, as well as engineers' drawings etched on Mylar using large graphic printers and airplane work breakdown structures. As task-level automation of existing manual systems was completed, Boeing developed further computer applications to integrate automated systems like payroll and accounts payable to support budgeting and product cost accounting.

With strong growth in Boeing's Commercial Airplane Division, management created branches for each of the major airplane programs. I was transferred to the 737 Branch as the 737 Financial Systems Manager. In this new job, my team and I created the 737 War Room, where we lined the walls with 737 work breakdown structures along with computer-generated reports for weekly 737 management meetings. At this point, Boeing had computer systems applications for reporting financial and cost accounting information and an ad hoc programming capability to generate rich information about factory performance and current airplane sales activity. Subsequently, the microcomputer era arrived, and Boeing was a leader in equipping its workers with computers on every desk. During this time, Boeing was also an early adopter of integrating legacy applications with emerging ERP (enterprise resource planning) software—the Baan ERP system.[2]

Subsequently, Boeing got bogged down in implementing the ERP system due to excessive modifications of the code to conform to the company's decentralized organization structure. Similar difficulties were incurred in Boeing's attempts to install a common CAD/CAM system across the corporation. In spite of these setbacks, Boeing's investments in IT continued to provide returns, as reflected in steady progress in increasing revenue per employee.

The 2016 vision and strategy (created in 1996) was developed in part to clarify what Boeing had to become to maintain industry leadership in the twenty-first century, and the Boeing Dreamliner (787) program was conceived as the impetus for a product-driven corporate transformation.

However, the decision to assimilate McDonnell-Douglas through a decentralized organizational structure stopped Boeing's corporate transformation dead in its tracks. Rather than integrating the two corporations through redesigned common corporate business processes, divisionalized business units were maintained along with diverse legacy IT systems from both the Boeing and McDonnell-Douglas corporations.

The increased organizational decentralization and the related choice to maintain legacy IT systems moved the company in the opposite direction from other leading corporations, such as IBM, that were also engaged in transformation. Under the leadership of CEO Lou Gerstner, IBM reengineered its legacy core IT systems into centralized corporate-wide integrated systems, enabling IBM to retool its inefficient operating cost structure to a competitive cost structure. This further facilitated IBM's transformation strategy to move from a manufacturing company to a customer service–driven IT systems integration company.

As articulated in its 2016 strategy, Boeing had a similar vision of transforming from a "wrench-turning Aerospace manufacturer" to a "large-scale Aerospace systems *integrator.*" But Boeing's road to transformation was different from IBM's. IBM started down the road of transformation at the enterprise level. In contrast, Boeing approached transformation through a product-driven model. The Boeing approach was intended to keep risk exposure in check by focusing first on creating a twenty-first-century organization for the new Dreamliner program, while maintaining uninterrupted major revenue streams from the other established programs. This part of the approach worked.

Second, the intention was to use the transformative learnings from the 787 program to guide the other business units into the new century. But the troubled execution of the 787 program slowed (if not stopped) the transformation of Boeing's other business units. While either the Boeing or IBM approach could have worked, Boeing's transformation was plagued by turmoil at the top and by unprecedented CEO leadership turnover.

The response to the 787 program's execution challenges was to pull back from the original vision in which Boeing was to hold a more limited role in design and manufacturing. Boeing engineers inserted themselves into the outsourcers' design and manufacturing activities to varying degrees. This led to confusion when the 787 manufacturing program ramped up to higher production rates. Ultimately, the resultant problems called into question the original intention to extend the 787's integrated global outsourcing strategy to other Boeing business units.

Apple represents another corporate transformation with certain similarities to both Boeing and IBM but with a different approach to execution. Apple co-founder and CEO, Steve Jobs, successfully pursued a vision of an easy to use personal computer (PC), embodied in the game-changing product: the Macintosh. As the company grew, Apple's board of directors convinced Jobs of the need for an operating executive to efficiently scale the organization to take advantage of Apple's opportunities. The board and Steve Jobs cooperated in hiring John Sculley from PepsiCo as CEO in 1983, and Jobs and Sculley worked as co-CEOs for a time, but then conflicts and disagreements arose.

The conflict led to a classic steward/creator power struggle and to a major fallout between Jobs and Sculley on new product development. After a showdown, the board chose Sculley over Jobs. Jobs departed from Apple in 1985 and sold all of his Apple stock.

Under Sculley's ten-year leadership, Apple grew from $800 million of revenue to $8 billion. But there were no successful new products developed to sustain Apple's growth. The Apple board replaced Sculley as CEO in 1993. Still lacking a new product pipeline under the new CEO, Apple bordered on the edge of bankruptcy.

Fortunately for Apple employees and shareholders, the downward spiral ended when the board invited Steve Jobs to come back. Jobs then took Apple back to his earlier vision of "ease of use" but further expanded the vision with the Mac computer as a systems hub for a person's phone, pictures, music, videos, movies, and books. This led to new products like the iPod and the iTunes music store, iPhone, and iPad. Jobs's leadership and new products and services propelled Apple to eclipse ExxonMobil in becoming the most valuable corporation in the world.

Similar to Boeing and IBM, Apple's vision under Steve Jobs was systems integration. All three corporations had grown for the most part organically until the late 1990s. In the late 1990s, Boeing's CEO, Phil Condit, made major acquisitions in space and defense; IBM's CEO, Lou Gerstner, acquired Lotus for its network business and then the PricewaterhouseCoopers consulting business. Apple made no major acquisitions, focusing instead on strategic partnerships, especially manufacturing in China.

Apple became a pioneer in exploiting the world's talent pool through strategic outsourcing. Steve Jobs had hired Deborah Coleman from Hewlett Packard in 1981 as Apple's financial controller. After several years, Coleman convinced Jobs to allow her to become VP of Apple's manufacturing. As the top manufacturing executive, Coleman led the development of Apple's highly automated advanced manufacturing process whereby the manufacturing line could be programmed to build any of several Apple computers as orders came in. This advanced manufacturing process was further refined for outsourcing to China. Internally, Apple focused on product development and marketing. As orders came in, they were outsourced to be manufactured in China, and the products were airlifted directly from the manufacturing facilities there to customers around the world in a matter of hours and days.

Boeing's product-driven transformation strategy involved aggressive strategic partnering in outsourcing major Tier 1 modules of the 787. Both Boeing and Apple adopted similar arguments about retaining the higher value-added activities while outsourcing lower-margin manufacturing tasks, as shown in the familiar laugh—or smiley curve[3] in Figure 8.1.

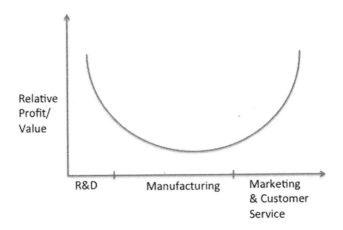

Figure 8.1   Relative Profit Margins for Product Design, Manufacturing, and Marketing

The strategic question is whether a corporation can retain the high margin activities in the longer run. For example, over time many large microchip manufacturing plants moved out of the United States and into Southeast Asia. China became very good at microchip manufacturing. But not satisfied to be stuck in low-margin manufacturing, these plants have continued to extend their capabilities.[4]

The Chinese manufacturing facilities became very good at employing CAD/CAM to rapidly prototype various microchip designs for products like the iPhone and other smartphones. These innovative skills have allowed the Chinese to migrate up both sides of the laugh curve toward higher-margin products. These capabilities became evident after the successful Chinese acquisition of IBM's PC business unit, renamed Lenovo. Lenovo has come out with new products and marketing programs that have proved successful in the global marketplace.

Some critics have described global outsourcing as the "hollowing out of American manufacturing," creating fierce competition from the outsourcing partners themselves.[5] Similar arguments were levied against Boeing's decision to sell its Wichita manufacturing plant to a Canadian group and the extensive outsourcing to global partners of the design and manufacture of 787 Tier 1 modules. Boeing's then-CEO responded that the decision would allow the Wichita plant to make parts for other airplane companies as well as for Boeing, thus enabling it to operate at full capacity, which was rarely achieved when Boeing was the plant's only customer. Under the new arrangement, the plant enjoyed lower per unit costs, passed the lower costs on to Boeing through lower prices, and everyone, including Boeing, could enjoy the benefits.

The challenge of global outsourcing continues to play out, and it is an extremely important one for corporations. Moreover, since the issue involves job availability and range of skills required, politics have come into play, further complicating the challenges for corporations. Nevertheless, the twenty-first-century strategies of Boeing, Apple, and IBM have assumed the inevitability of globalization and the validity of being able to operate successfully in an environment of virtually integrated corporations including global strategic partners.

OTIS ELEVATOR: A CLASSIC EXAMPLE

Otis Elevator, now a subsidiary of United Technologies Corporation (UTC), is another transformation model worthy of analysis and contrast. With almost 90 percent of its 60,000 employees working outside the United States, Otis transformed from a highly globalized twentieth-century manufacturing company to an IT-enabled twenty-first-century service company.

Otis Elevator was founded 1853, in Yonkers, New York, by Elisha Graves Otis, who invented the "safety brake elevator." Since then, the activities of Otis have spanned more than 150 years in the design, manufacture, and servicing of elevators around the world.[6]

Otis was fueled by a vision of providing high-rise elevators to enable the great cities of the world to grow vertically versus continued horizontal growth. Upon reaching $1 billion in revenue in the 1970s, with more than half of its revenue coming from outside the United States, Otis was acquired by United Technologies (UTC) and grew to exceed $11 billion of revenue, as the company drew on its fellow UTC high-tech companies to strategically integrate solid state technologies into its products, thereby fighting back threatening competition from outside competitors. By 2004, 1.5 million Otis elevators and 100,000 Otis escalators were in service all over the world.

George David, CEO of UTC in the early 2000s, had led an organizational transformation at Otis in the 1980s, when he was COO there. That earlier transformation rested on the establishment of an IT-enabled centralized customer service system, called OTISLINE, to dispatch elevator service mechanics for repairs.

OTISLINE introduced centralized reporting and tracking for each service incident. When an elevator failed, building personnel called OTISLINE, and the event was logged at a computer console. An operator then assigned the repair call to a specific mechanic in an appropriate branch. The mechanic was dispatched to the elevator site. After the mechanic had done the work and while still on site, he sent back an electronic OTISLINE report summarizing the results of the work, and the central database was updated.

This created a very large database of elevator service calls, time to repair situations, and inadequacies or problems with the repair. Analysis of this database allowed the company to quickly understand which offices were delivering fast, reliable service, and which ones were not, as well as which elevator models were giving major repair difficulties, and which ones were not.[7]

A second important IT-enabled strategic initiative during the 1980s was the move to remote elevator monitoring (REM). A product innovation that enabled new service capabilities, REM involved building into elevators a microprocessor to log statistics, which communicate to headquarters in real time about the performance of an in-service elevator. These reports were used to foresee problems with elevators and to dispatch service mechanics before an elevator failed. The REM capability helped Otis compete in the service business through a capability many of its competitors, especially smaller service companies, could not imitate.

George David handpicked Otis's new president in 2002, Ari Bousbib. Bousbib believed that being a great service company meant more than just delivering flawless performance for units under maintenance. His often repeated mantra: "We maintain elevators, we service customers."

Bousbib argued that Otis needed to redefine its processes beyond service support tools such as OTISLINE and REM. Bousbib described a program for achieving fivefold improvement in the order-to-hand-over cycle within five years. Similar to David's earlier approach, Bousbib relied on business processes and technologies as instruments of change.

The main lesson of the Otis case is the importance of "hands-on" CEOs leading a major IT transformation effort, where everything from technical to process changes are extremely difficult—especially in a successful legacy company reinventing itself for the global challenges of the twenty-first century.

The Otis case also supports getting an early start in the shift from traditional twentieth-century "make-and-sell" manufacturing organizations to strategically responsive customer-driven companies—the twenty-first-century "sense-and-respond" competitive imperative. This transformation is much harder for successful traditional manufacturing companies than for greenfield companies founded in the IT-enabled network environments of the twenty-first century.

SIMILARITIES AND DIFFERENCES IN BEING AND BECOMING TWENTY-FIRST-CENTURY CORPORATIONS

The challenges of being or becoming a twenty-first-century corporation vary greatly based upon the company's age, history, industry, executive leadership, and competitive threats. The faster growth of companies like Amazon typically yields much higher revenue per employee compared to a transforming company like Otis, with revenue per employee barely exceeding $100,000. The road to transformation for legacy companies is much longer and requires a lot of time and persistent CEO leadership.

Indeed, the greenfield environments and timing of Amazon and Google had real advantages over corporations that have been forced to change from established twentieth-century corporations to twenty-first-century corporations. Also, both Amazon and Google were led by CEOs who grew up in the rich digital IT environment. As "digital natives," the founders and CEOs at Amazon and Google saw IT as a natural and familiar resource ripe for exploitation. They embraced IT unreservedly, sought out locations in IT-friendly environments like Silicon Valley and Seattle, and hired digital natives like themselves.

In contrast, twentieth-century corporations were typically led by "digital immigrants"—those who did not grow up with IT but who had to learn it at a more advanced age. For some, this may have seemed similar to learning a foreign language well after childhood, when language acquisition is at its peak. With such a disadvantage, it is a lot harder to think in terms of IT opportunities, threats, and processes. Accordingly, those digital immigrant CEOs face an inherent challenge in transforming their organizations into successful twenty-first-century corporations. In addition, the twentieth-century corporations are not likely to be in an IT-friendly environment like Silicon Valley or Seattle, where mutually supportive elements such as active high-tech ventures offer a natural flow of talented IT professionals attracted to anchor companies like Hewlett-Packard, Google, and Microsoft. Aligned with major research universities such as Stanford and the University of Washington, these activities provide a steady source of talented and trained entry-level workers and advanced research, including the IT research emanating from the well-known Computer Science departments at Stanford and the University of Washington.

So we see two early examples of corporations that have exploited from the outset their opportunities to be twenty-first-century corporations. Jeff Bezos created Amazon to build on all the opportunities that twenty-first-century technology could offer. Larry Page and Sergey Brin founded Google on the basis of twenty-first-century innovations. Search had already emerged as a viable Internet product or service and was dominated by Yahoo! until Brin and Page innovated and commercialized a significantly better search engine. The new and superior search engine was rapidly discovered by Internet users and gained almost an instant following. Almost overnight Google became the search industry leader. In the twenty-first-century competitive environment, customers can be a click away from departing a corporation. Continuously, traditional management concepts are being challenged, such as "stickiness" of customers to a brand and overcoming customer switching costs.

Successful twentieth-century corporations face challenges that greenfield companies like Amazon, Google, and Apple can avoid. It can be a bit treacherous for legacy organizations to adopt greenfield models without careful consideration of the company's traditional sources of success. Nevertheless, the greenfield sites can offer insights on what the end point of transformed corporations might be. Perhaps the most important learning is one we covered in chapter 5, about the need to rethink the process of innovations and those that create innovations in corporations.

Three factors often impede twentieth-century corporations' progress toward renewing the success patterns they have enjoyed during most of their history: past history of success, persistence of outmoded CEO leadership, and lack of strategic IT leadership.

Past Success

Past history of success is one of the most difficult and frequently experienced factors to overcome. CEO Lou Gerstner at IBM got so frustrated in hearing about the earlier IBM successes that he emblazoned a T-shirt and gave it to executives who went on and on about their earlier successes: "The older I get the better I was."

It often takes an uncontrolled corporate crisis such as steady and deep financial losses to shock the workforce into embracing the cultural changes required to move away from the old way of doing things and embrace different ways of working that are more appropriate for succeeding in the new competitive environment.

Outmoded Leadership

A second factor is persistence of outmoded CEO leadership. A transformative vision and strategy are extremely important to effective CEO leadership, but transformation can be stopped dead in its tracks without effective hands-on CEO leadership during execution. This kind of leadership is highly collaborative and cannot be carried out by remote control—whether it be across geographical or organizational distance, where communications have to travel through layers and layers of organization structure.

In addition, different CEO leaders might be needed at different times. As we observed in the Boeing case, the company had been led by a series of CEOs who were right for their times. CEO Frank Shrontz led Boeing for ten years (1986–1996) to become a $37 billion revenue company with its highest share price breaking the $100 mark, which did not reoccur until June 7, 2013. Shrontz and the board selected his successor in 1996, Phil Condit, applying a vetting process that had evolved and proved effective from the time that Boeing had reached $1 billion in revenue. Shrontz charged Phil Condit with assembling a team to develop a vision and strategy that would extend Boeing's industry leadership into the twenty-first century. Condit's team's strategy remains Boeing's strategy going forward today.

Phil Condit created an excellent vision and set the company on a good strategy. But there are three essential ingredients for transformation: vision and strategy are nothing without effective execution. Condit's execution was fraught with distractions and missteps, finally leading to his removal by the board. The board chose the former McDonnell-Douglas CEO and then Boeing board member, Harry Stonecipher, to succeed Condit. Stonecipher erred by insisting on extended global outsourcing at the outset for the 787 program. He only lasted fifteen months and was replaced by the board with Boeing board member James McNerney.

McNerney got off to a rocky start by leading the execution of the highly promising Dreamliner program from afar after the move of the Boeing Corporate Headquarters from Seattle to Chicago. Boeing had earlier contracted to deliver 787s to the Chinese airlines in time to fly spectators to the 2008 Summer Olympics—an auspicious inroad into one of the most important growing markets for commercial airlines in the twenty-first century. It was a strategic error to delay the official disclosure of well-known early 787 outsourcing problems to airline customers and shareholders.

In the midst of scrambling to get the Dreamliner program on track, union negotiations broke down. Soon afterward, Boeing made a strategic decision not to build a second 787 final assembly line next to the Everett final assembly line but rather 3,000 miles away in right-to-work state South Carolina. Recruiting and training a new workforce there resulted in learning curve problems that increased the risk of further delivery delays.

The Dreamliner program continued to spiral downward until it became the most troubled Boeing new airplane program ever, when the FAA grounded the in-service 787 fleet soon after FAA certification. Seething cultural problems came to the surface when Boeing's machinist union members voted to reject Boeing's offer for an eight-year extension of the union contract. Upon the rejection, Boeing immediately solicited offers from other states to build factories for Boeing's new 777-X aircraft to weigh against building the 777-X at the existing 777 Everett factory. Boeing received offers from twenty-two states, some of which offered billions of dollars in subsidies.

With the potential loss of more than 10,000 jobs in Washington State, political pressure mounted. Boeing promised to do final assembly of its 777-X, including the plane's composite wings, in the Puget Sound region if the machinists approved the eight-year contract extension. Washington's state legislature approved $8.7 billion in subsidies for Boeing through 2040 if Boeing placed 777-X final assembly in Washington State. On January 3, 2014, union members re-voted. Fifty-one percent approved the eight-year extension, which also included a provision that the union would not strike during the life of the contract.

After nine years of McNerney's CEO tenure at Boeing, the results have been mixed. Most importantly, the 787 Dreamliner has been certified and entered into the world's airline fleets. Nevertheless, the delivery of 787 airplanes has been anything but smooth, and factions at Boeing remain in conflict. The strong traditional Boeing company culture remains fractured without the emergence of an equally strong integrated corporate culture for the new century.

After a long period of leadership from afar, together with successive costly delivery delays for the 787 program, McNerney gave signs of seizing direct hands-on leadership to solve the 787 battery fire safety issues, get the FAA grounding ban lifted, and return the 787s to the skies. It is remarkable that during the troubled times, few airlines canceled their orders, and the record commercial airplane sales of the Dreamliner remained largely intact—testament to Boeings leading strategic capabilities in the design and manufacture of industry game-changing commercial airplanes.

The twenty-first century is proving to be an exceedingly challenging time for CEOs, and it will be left to history to judge James McNerney's performance as Boeing's CEO leader during these transformative times.

Inadequate CEO Leadership for Strategic IT Development

A third factor has to do with effective executive leadership in establishing the necessary IT capabilities to drive the transformation. This requires shifting IT resource management from strictly tactical to mission-critical and strategic. Too many twentieth-century corporations undermanage IT. This can lead to situations whereby IT strategic leadership is "everywhere and nowhere," as discussed in chapter 6. A contributing problem is that the current ranks of CEO corporate leaders are more likely to be digital immigrants than digital natives.

The Cisco transformation is a good example of an effective way to address this problem. Cisco was an early innovator in the IT technologies that enabled the Internet, which, in turn, resulted in an explosive demand for Cisco products. With the increased demand, Cisco quickly incurred problems with its legacy manufacturing systems leading to the total shutdown of its factories. John Mortgridge, then CEO and a digital immigrant, responded by trusting his CIO, Pete Solvik, to collaborate in solving Cisco's IT problem.

Mortgridge hired Solvik as a promising young CIO. Not only did Mortgridge establish a strong relationship with Solvik by spending time with him and mentoring him, but Mortgridge went beyond that by lining up directorship positions for Solvik in other Silicon Valley companies. Morgridge's intention was not only to mentor Solvik on strategic business issues but also to give him firsthand experience in dealing with the issues in other companies as a board member. Mortgridge's investment paid off when Cisco's unprecedented product growth required a complete strategic revamping of its IT systems infrastructure,[8] which Solvik accomplished in close collaboration with Mortgridge and the rest of the executive team.

Otis's story was similar to Cisco's but differed in that it was not triggered by a crisis but as a relatively long-term evolution from a successful twentieth-century manufacturing corporation into a twenty-first-century customer service corporation—a transformation that is still underway.

Two digital immigrant CEOs played major roles in the transformation of Otis. The first CEO was George David, who led Otis from an excessively decentralized corporation to a successful IT-enabled centralized, but functional, global organization with the IT OTISLINE initiative. The second CEO was Ari Bousbib, who built on OTISLINE and continued the transformation of Otis with an IT-enabled initiative of transforming Otis from a manufacturing company to a customer service company.

Otis's more gradual transformation from a successful twentieth-century corporation to a successful twenty-first-century corporation seems to be more typical than the crisis-driven transformation that confronted Cisco. The older and bigger the corporation, the longer it takes for a successful transformation.

Cisco CEO John Mortgridge possessed two key characteristics necessary for leading the transformation of a twentieth-century corporation to a twenty-first-century corporation. First is the characteristic of recognizing the need for transformational change. Second is the characteristic of knowing what you don't know and doing something about it. Here Mortgridge knew that strategic management of IT was essential to the transformation of Cisco. He also knew that he did not know the processes for strategic implementation of IT well enough to consummate a transformation. He knew that he had to acquire the capability of knowing. This led to the importance of securing someone who had IT understanding and IT management capabilities beyond his own.

Mortgridge recognized that Pete Solvik was that person he needed and also that he himself would never have the IT understanding and IT management capabilities needed to undertake the IT-enabled transformation of Cisco. Accordingly, he engaged in building trust and a peer-to-peer collaborative relationship with Solvik. Even more important, Mortgridge engaged in an "outward bound" mentoring program to help Solvik acquire what the Harvard Business School once called the "administrative point of view"— that is, the ability to think like a CEO.

Solvik commented to me how valuable this experience was in rounding him out as a full participating member of Mortgridge's executive team, as well as helping him understand how to present and work with the Cisco board of directors through the many critical decisions involved in the transformation of Cisco, in particular regarding investments in strategic IT capabilities.

TRANSFORMATIVE LEADERSHIP: THE CRITICAL ROLES OF CEOS AND DIRECTORS

Few CEOs have been as prescient as John Mortgridge about what it takes to transform a corporation. Fewer still have been able to build a collaborative partnership between themselves and their CIOs or whoever was needed to become a trusted partner in the corporate transformation team.

This kind of collaborative partnership went missing at Boeing. It was the fiduciary responsibility of the Boeing board's oversight to detect this omission and take appropriate action. Unfortunately, a collaborative partnership or effective board oversight did not happen. In chapter 9 we delve into the board of directors' responsibilities with respect to the transformation to twenty-first-century corporations, and we discuss how to ensure that these oversight responsibilities are met.

NOTES

1. A "digital native" is someone who has grown up in a rich environment of IT, and the term is contrasted with "digital immigrants", which means those who were born earlier and have not grown up with IT—digital immigrants have had to learn IT similar to the process of having to learn a new foreign language. This is where the phrase originated for the natural, easy use of IT: "as the air we breathe."
2. The Baan Corporation was created by Jan Baan in 1978 in Barneveld, Netherlands. With the development of his first software package, Jan Baan and his brother, Paul Baan, entered what was to become the ERP (enterprise resource planning) industry.
3. Uses of simple graphics such as a circle containing two dots for eyes and a curve for the mouth came to be well known as the smiley face. The smiley face was created in 1963 by Harvey Ball for an insurance company in Massachusetts. This design was a bright yellow circle representing a face, with black oval eyes and a big curved mouth with smile creases at the ends. The familiar smiley face has been used in the illustration of a number of concepts including the representation in Figure 8.1 to show relative profit margins for outsourcers of stage activities of product development, manufacturing, and marketing.
4. Interestingly, Apple's CEO, Tim Cook, announced to ABC News on December 6, 2012, that Apple planned to bring some manufacturing back to the United States from China for their Mac computers. Cook also stated that other manufacturing would have to remain in China because of the unique skills that were in China but not available in the United States. Also reported in Rampell, Catherine, and Wingfield, Nick, "In Shift of Jobs, Apple Will Make Some Macs in U.S.," *The New York Times*, December 7, 2012, p. 1.
5. July 8, 2012, "The Hollowing Out" by Thomas B. Edsall, *New York Times, Opinions*, http://campaignstops.blogs.nytimes.com/2012/07/08/the-future-of-joblessness/?_php=true&_type=blogs&_r=0, accessed September 15, 2014.
6. *Otis: Giving Rise to the Modern City* by Jason Goodwin (Chicago: Ivan R. Dee, 2001) provides a historical account of the founding and evolution of the Otis Corporation through multiple business cycles and CEOs. This book provides rich context for this case study of an integration stage.
7. Although not referred to as "big data" at the time, Otis was a global pioneer in exploiting its IT-enabled "big data" asset long before the term came into vogue.
8. See the Cisco HBS case on Cisco by Austin, Cotteleer, and Nolan, which describes Cisco's successful ERP initiative in replacing Cisco's entire IT systems infrastructure.

BIBLIOGRAPHY

Austin, Robert, Cotteleer, Mark D., and Nolan, Richard L., "Cisco Systems, Inc.: Implementing ERP," HBS Case #9–699–022. Revised May 6, 2002.
Goodwin, Jason, *Otis: Giving Rise to the Modern City* (Chicago: Ivan R. Dee, 2001).

9 Twenty-First-Century Imperatives for Boards and Senior Executives

The modern corporation has emerged into the twenty-first century as a marvel for creating economic value at a magnitude never seen before, but not without controversy and dangers. Contrasting the "then" and "now" corporate competitive environment, as we did in chapter 2, suggests that the size and global complexity of twenty-first-century corporations have outpaced the development of their corporate boards of directors. The mismatch between what is and what is needed leads to the conclusion that nothing short of a complete rethinking and reinventing the board can bridge the gap.

Like the corporation itself, the corporate board of directors has evolved as a work in process. The current state of boards, however, reflects a stilted state of development in which weak boards often fail to carry out their duties of oversight of corporate leadership and performance. It is instructive to trace the evolution of boards with the rise of the corporation and in order to understand how boards generally operate today and how they could be reinvented to become more effective.

THE DEVELOPMENT OF CORPORATE BOARDS OF DIRECTORS

The evolution of the Boeing Company board of directors typifies that of many corporations that grew up during the twentieth century. As at Boeing, the roots of directors' committees were usually the executive committees and included the executive management responsible for leading the main functional areas of engineering, manufacturing, sales, and accounting.

Young corporations on the road to success required significant investment funds, which at some point exceeded the internal cash-generating capacity of the corporation, and/or the means of the founding entrepreneur. During Boeing's Stage 1 of corporate growth, Bill Boeing added two outside professionals to the meetings of his executive committee to advise him and his team on recruiting additional investors to fund Boeing's expansion: a Seattle lawyer and a Seattle banker. This expanded committee met periodically, leading to Boeing's early form of a board of directors. It eventually was formalized into a standing committee.

This early form for boards of directors continued until 1934, when the Securities and Exchange (SEC) Act was enacted to provide federal regulation of corporations and strengthen the workings of the capital markets by curtailing abuses, such as misleading stock offerings and unfair competitive practices. The federal regulations required more complete and accurate disclosure from corporations selling financial instruments to the public. Most importantly, the act included a requirement that outside professionally accredited auditors certify the corporations' annual financial performance reports and provide a formal auditor's opinion that the financial performance was fairly reported and disclosed according to Generally Accepted Accounting Principles (GAAP).

The SEC Act and agency were part of newly elected U.S. President Franklin Delano Roosevelt's New Deal program. Roosevelt selected Joseph Kennedy, a successful and respected businessman, to lead the SEC and serve as its first chairman. Kennedy was instrumental in convincing executives of the need for regulation in order for corporations to have access to the public capital markets that would provide the financial resources required for growth throughout the economy. In addition, the public stock exchanges such as the New York and American stock exchanges established requirements for corporations that listed their stocks on the exchanges.

With the departure of Bill Boeing and the restructuring of the company, Boeing's 1934 board of directors committee was restructured and further formalized. From the mid-1930s through the 1950s, the board's schedule evolved to include four or five all-day meetings sequenced throughout the calendar year. Formal board charters emerged along with a set of formal subcommittees including the audit committee, the compensation committee, and the governance committee. More board members were recruited to serve as independent outside directors and chairmen of the subcommittees. Within the same time period, corporate boards of directors in general followed similar patterns in developing their structures and memberships.

By 1960, the Boeing board numbered thirteen, with six outside directors and seven inside directors. The inside directors were steeped in aeronautical engineering and accounting experience. The outside directors were CEOs and chairmen of other manufacturing and financial services corporations.

By 1990, the Boeing board counted several interlocking directorships. The eleven board members served on an average of 4.6 boards each, and a number of the directors served on many of the same corporate boards. Boeing CEO Frank Shrontz served on CEO John Ferry's Boise Cascade board. Boeing's prior CEO and board chairman, T Wilson, served on CEO George Weyerhaeuser's board, as did Chevron CEO Harold Haynes (previously Boeing's CFO) and PACCAR CEO Charles Pigott. Harold Haynes and George Keller, both retired chairmen and CEOs of Chevron, had recruited George Shultz and Charles Pigott on to the Chevron board. Charles Pigott had Harold Haynes, George Weyerhaeuser, and T Wilson served on the PACCAR board.

The often-cited advantage of having chairmen and CEOs serving on each other's boards of directors was that each gets to know intimately the issues that the other chairmen and CEOs are facing and can provide relevant shared experiences for addressing the issues. The disadvantages included moral hazard: "you scratch my back, I scratch yours." In other words, if CEOs serve on each other's boards, there could be a temptation to be less than diligent in scrutinizing each other's leadership and compensation packages.

In 2000, Phil Condit was Boeing's chairman and CEO. The thirteen-member board consisted of eleven outside directors[1] and two inside directors (Phil Condit and Harry Stonecipher, President and Chief Operating Officer). Although Condit served as a Hewlett-Packard director, and Lew Platt, Retired H-P chairman and CEO, served on the Boeing board, the interlocking of directors that existed in 1990 had been largely eliminated in response to heavy pressure from shareholders and shareholder advocates, part of the trend toward having the majority of the board members being outside, independent directors. Downside risks accompanied the trend toward outside directors, however. The most obvious side effect was that the board lost members who really understood the corporation's business.

The further development of boards of directors seemed to become stilted around the turn of the century. In the United States, the majority of corporate boards maintained the practice of having the CEO also serve as board chairperson. This provided the CEO the basis for wielding power and influence in selecting board members as well as having sway over the board meeting agenda.

By 2000, Condit was the only Boeing board member with aeronautical engineering expertise. The Boeing board also was characterized by lopsided stock holdings. John McDonnell held about 1.5 million shares of Boeing stock, and Harry Stonecipher held 936,000 shares. The next biggest owner was Phil Condit with 440,000 shares. All three would stand to directly benefit in the short run from any financial engineering such as expense cutting or avoidance of risky new airplane development programs.

In late 2003, the board removed Condit and elected Harry Stonecipher CEO. Board member Lew Platt was elected chairman of the board. In early 2004, the board debated giving their final approval to the Dreamliner program. Stonecipher was rumored to insist that the board acquiesce to extreme cost shifting through outsourcing as a condition to board approval of the 787 new airplane program. The board went on to approve going forward with the program.

Within a short fifteen months, Stonecipher was fired by the board. James Bell, the CFO, was appointed interim CEO, while the board conducted a search, and finally appointed in 2005 one of their own directors, Jim McNerney, as Chairman and CEO.[2]

Lew Platt served as lead director until his untimely death a few months after McNerney became CEO. During McNerney's chairmanship, seven directors were replaced with five new directors. The Boeing 2014 board consisted of eleven directors, none of whom had any formal aerospace or commercial airplane engineering or manufacturing experience. John McDonnell was not carried over from the 2000 board.[3]

With the exception of John McDonnell's[4] formal background several years earlier, experience in aeronautical engineering was absent from this board. Board-level understanding and experience in providing effective advice and oversight on highly technological and complex new airplane programs like the 787 was either missing or weak at best.

Boards that lack background and experience on the subject matter of corporations involved in highly technical and complex products like commercial airplanes tend to be excessively conservative. This problem can significantly worsen if CEO chairmen with conflicts of interest exert excessive control over information presented to the directors. The conflict can be further exacerbated when general collegiality and board dynamics discourage questions or challenges that might offend other board members. In such circumstances, some refer to board meetings as "social loafing." The atmosphere can gravitate to excessive compromise and mediocre outcomes when the board votes on important issues such as new airplane programs and manufacturing strategies.

REINVENTING OF THE BOARD OF DIRECTORS: THE TIPPING POINT

The mythical straw that breaks the camel's back and leads to a massive movement, or tipping point, to reinvent corporate boards of directors is likely to be runaway CEO compensation. By 2010, the rising ripples over CEO compensation had grown into a dangerous rogue wave.

The New York Times had Equilar, an executive compensation data firm, conduct an independent study of two hundred large corporations that showed the average worker in the United States had a 2010 median annual compensation of $41,674, an increase of 2 percent from the average $40,712 the previous year.[5] The average CEO compensation was $9,600,000—a 12 percent increase. Commentators noted that the highly publicized 1950 Great Brinks Robbery[6]—the largest robbery in U.S. history at the time—netted the perpetrators only $1.2 million.

In 2010 a number of CEOs did even better than 12 percent increases. CEO Philippe Dauman of Viacom received a pay raise of 149 percent for a total of $84.5 million; at Stanley Black & Decker, CEO John Lundgren's pay increase was 253 percent for a total of $32.6 million; and U.S. Bancorp CEO Richard Davis received an increase of 143 percent for a total of $16.1 million. Overall public reaction was understandably negative at a time of very high U.S. unemployment rates and flat corporate profits.

It had become commonplace for CEO compensation to go beyond the limits of good judgment and even beyond the law in CEO enrichment.[7] Outraged American lawmakers[8] had attempted to rein in excess CEO compensation with regulations and laws such as the decade-old Sarbanes-Oxley legislation.[9] But there was only so much that legislation could do, and there was the risk that if legislation went overboard, as many claimed that Sarbanes-Oxley had, the effects would be damaging to the corporation itself.[10]

More typically than not, such government regulations and shareholders' legal actions have resulted in little benefits to shareholders but significant monies for the plaintiff and defendant lawyers and law firms associated with writing the legislation and executing the lawsuits. And the regulations led to boom times for consulting and public accounting firms as corporations saw their already substantial auditing fees double.

The debate went on about disclosing directors' approach and methodologies for determining executive compensation. The legislation went only so far as to allow shareholders an advisory vote on the corporation's CEO and executive compensation proposals.[11] Nevertheless, shareholder advisory votes increasingly expressed displeasure with CEO and executive compensation packages, and especially with "golden parachutes" for removed or fired CEOs and executives. On March 23, 2011, Hewlett-Packard shareholders cast 50 percent of their shares against H-P's executive compensation program. H-P was criticized for having their CEO on the board's governance committee, while the governance committee went about restructuring the board with five new directors. This happened just after the previous CEO was removed in August 2010 over inaccurate expense reports involving his personal relationship with an H-P contractor.

The trend toward excessive CEO compensation along with weak board oversight has reached a point that in all too many corporations it has become a dysfunctional flash point. For example, after Boeing's 777-X new airplane program was approved by the board on May 1, 2013, 259 airplane airline orders flooded in for a total list price of $95 billion.[12] Later, Boeing negotiations with its Washington State machinist union broke down over an impasse on replacing the current machinist employee pension plan with a less attractive 401(k) employee contribution plan. Boeing threatened to move 777-X manufacturing out of the state of Washington to another state. The union responded that this threat was retaliatory, unfair, and simply inequitable with disclosure that CEO James McNerney's Boeing pension plan had reached a level of $265,000 per month.

Perceived inequity had reached deeply into the Boeing Corporation. What had been a relatively amicable and positive relationship between Boeing and its professional engineers had become contentious. Over sixty-six years of SPEEA[13] union affiliation for Boeing's engineering employees, there had been no strikes during the twentieth century, and only one in the twenty-first—a forty-day action in 2000. However, SPEEA seemed to move further from Boeing management and closer to the machinists after the 2001 executive decision to relocate Boeing's headquarters from Seattle to Chicago, and the 2009 executive decision to build the second 787 airplane final assembly plant not in Everett, Washington, but in Charleston, South Carolina, recruiting a nonunion workforce there.

I do not suggest that resolving the current situation will be easy or quick by any means. I remember all too well the rather hostile response my colleague, HBS Professor Michael Jensen, an authority on the CEO and moral hazard, received from CEOs and senior executives in the 1990s when he talked about the subject at the Harvard Business School Executive Education programs.[14] Many of these executives believed that their compensation packages were not at all excessive. They often argued that the high compensation was simply market forces at work, and that the third party compensation advisory firms hired by their boards of directors' compensation committees provided corroborative evidence.[15] The more they argued and the more research Professor Jensen provided, the more hostile the discussion became.

Professors Max Bazerman (Harvard Business School) and Ann Tenbrunsel (Notre Dame University) have researched this phenomenon and concluded that unethical conduct tends to occur when people unconsciously fool themselves.[16] The authors state:

> In addition to preventing us from noticing our own unethical conduct, ethical fading causes us to overlook the unethical behavior of others. In the run-up to the financial crisis, corporate boards, auditing firms, credit-rating agencies and other parties had easy access to damning data that they should have noticed and reported. Yet they didn't do so, at least in part because of "motivated blindness"—the tendency to overlook information that works against one's best interest. Ample research shows that people who have a vested self-interest, even the most honest among us, have difficulty being objective.[17] Worse yet, they often fail to recognize their lack of objectivity.[18]

The U.S. Senate Permanent Subcommittee on Investigations' 650-page report, "Wall Street and the Financial Crisis," published on April 13, 2011, describes how as the mortgage crisis widened, two risk managers at the failed Washington Mutual Bank were fired by the CEO after they told regulators that the loss estimates provided to the regulators by Washington Mutual executives were outdated.[19] The firing of a risk manager by the CEO should be a red flag subject to disclosure, similar to the firing of a corporation's CFO. In the Washington Mutual case, it wasn't.

BOARD OVERSIGHT FOR ALL OF THE CORPORATION'S STRATEGIC ASSETS

The board of directors has fiduciary responsibilities for providing oversight on the management of all the corporation's assets. In the twenty-first century, IT has enabled a new and severely underexploited corporate strategic asset: the information asset. Corporate IT management presents a sad story of misunderstanding and neglect that too often keeps boards from recognizing or reaping the potential returns from such a valuable frozen asset.

The broad business adoption and the ensuing explosive growth of the Internet in the last years of the twentieth century underscore the new strategic potential of IT. The 787 program shows the potential for coupling IT and digitization to enable global virtual integration in creating a sophisticated product. Four lessons about potential IT benefits and their capture can be drawn from the Boeing 787 experience:

- IT plus "digitization" create unique new ways to achieve competitive advantages a) through virtual, organizational integration that can offer management a razor focus on core capabilities, and b) through accessing a diverse and uniquely talented global workforce.
- The effective management and coordination of a global, virtually integrated organization is a newly emerging challenge, still fraught with risks that require serious board-level oversight.
- IT plus "digitization" will likely continue to have a major impact on the changing nature of work, and with global expansion, on where and how work is done.
- Culture clashes and other organizational effects that result in loss of, or failure to bring to bear, integration skills can generate very substantial difficulties in efforts to use IT to create new capabilities and value.

Long ago the role of IT in corporations shifted from supporting business strategies to being an integral part of business strategies. As shown in the Boeing case, strategic IT can't be simply functionalized and positioned into the traditional twentieth-century organization structures to enjoy the full strategic benefits of IT investments.

In Boeing, "IT was everywhere," and "IT strategic leadership was fleetingly, nowhere." Similarly, IT leadership and decision making have too frequently become so fragmented and dissipated in twenty-first-century global networks that formulating coherent corporate IT strategies has become an exceedingly elusive enterprise. This elusiveness contributed to the unprecedented three-and-a-half year delivery delay of Boeing's 787 airplane—an extremely expensive lesson to be learned.

While the CIO's position is now often viewed as similar in importance to the CFO's—certainly a step in the right direction—the role of CIO is comparatively immature in most corporations. Similar to the stereotype of the CFO as the "numbers guy" before the Enron fiasco and bankruptcy, CIOs have been too often dismissed and stereotyped as the "IT geeks."[20]

In the Boeing 787 case, the strategic IT issues were subtle. Boeing was a leader in many aspects of IT, but overall strategic thinking about the role of IT and its opportunities seemingly went missing upon the departure of Phil

Condit as CEO. And there was no board oversight to call attention to this omission. The "elephant" in the Boeing board room, as well in the board rooms of many other modern corporations, is ubiquitous IT spread throughout the corporation but without strategic focus and leadership.

I have participated in establishing two board-level technology committees, including drafting committee charters, recruiting committee members, and selecting committee chairs. In a jointly authored *Harvard Business Review* article, my colleague Professor Warren McFarlan and I presented our arguments for IT board-level oversight, based in part on our own experiences as board members dealing with corporate IT oversight issues.[21]

Since our *HBR* article was published in 2005, the issues of IT board-level oversight regarding strategic opportunities and risks have become even more important and urgent. A joint survey of more than two hundred board directors conducted by the National Association of Corporate Directors and the Oliver Wyman Global Risk Center found 47 percent of the directors surveyed dissatisfied with their boards' ability to provide IT risk oversight.[22] Explosive trends in smartphones (like the iPhone and Android phones and the powerful apps that now are available for smartphones), and "cloud computing," where corporate data leaves the premises of the corporate data center to "live" remotely in the ether, raise security and competitive issues requiring careful board deliberations.[23]

NEW RISKS AND CHALLENGES

Boeing's experience in strategically transforming to the twenty-first-century competition and expansive global environment holds insights about the risks and challenges that CEO executive teams and corporate boards must face.

Dysfunctional Legal Systems

First is the risk of serious dysfunctions in twentieth-century legacy institutions, such as the U.S. legal system's inherent propensity to exploit unfortunate disastrous events, which are highly correlated with extraordinary large jury settlements. Both pre-jury as well as jury trials typically result in multimillion-dollar settlements that enrich law firms more than the plaintiffs who have experienced real suffering and loss.

The March 8, 2014, tragic loss of Malaysian Flight 370 Boeing 777/200ER somewhere over the Indian Ocean with all passengers and crew presumed dead is an example. In spite of the incredible safety record of the Boeing 777 in being the safest plane in the history of commercial air travel, it did not take long for lawyers to convince family members to bring lawsuits for their tragic losses against the Boeing Corporation where the "deep pockets" money is.

These types of lawsuits initiate a long and expensive legal process that engages armies of lawyers and "experts" beginning with a "petition of discovery." The Malaysian Flight 370 petition for discovery was filed in a Cook County, Illinois, Circuit Court mere days after Flight 370 went missing. The lawsuit discovery was meant to secure evidence of possible design and manufacturing defects that may have contributed to the disaster. It will inevitably produce thousands upon thousands of documents, which then will engage lawyers reading through the documents preparing hundreds and hundreds of briefs, responses to the briefs, and on and on.

The law firm that initiated the suit petitioned the court to order Boeing to provide the identity of manufacturers of various plane components, including electric components and wiring, batteries, emergency oxygen, and fire alarm systems. It also seeks the identity of the company or person who last inspected the fuselage and those who provided maintenance, along with information about crew training for catastrophic incidents, security practices, safety training, crew evaluations, and more.

Boeing most certainly will have purchased D&O (directors and officers) insurance against the risk of being sued. In the United States, approximately $2 billion of premium D&O insurance is written each year, providing an average of $140 million to $200 million in coverage for lawsuits against the directors and officers of corporations. In addition, it is common that the corporation indemnifies corporate directors and officers against the expenses of being personally sued regarding their corporate work, and provides "excess coverage" policies to cover expenses if the corporation should become bankrupt. About one third of public corporations have had one or more D&O insurance claims in the last ten years.

Generally, the lawsuits continue for long periods. After a time generally associated with the defendant's insurance policies limits running out, the lawyers agree to settle the suit for some undisclosed amount. Typically the largest percentage of the settlement goes to the lawyers and their firms, and a much smaller percentage of the settlement is directly paid to the parties named in the lawsuit.

All of this has resulted in excessive expenses that companies like Boeing have felt compelled to pass on as the "cost of doing business."

Ineffective Management and Entrenched Twentieth-Century Cultures

Second is the risk of ineffective management and the legacy of embedded corporate cultures of the twentieth century. There is a lot that we still do not know about the General Motors executive decisions not to correct the ignition switches in certain Chevrolet cars (for less than $1.00 per car) that allegedly led to the deaths of thirteen Chevrolet car owners and an overall recall of more than 20 million GM cars and trucks. But what we do know is that while General Motors shareholders will shoulder the cost of any fines or settlements, and the more intangible but significant costs are those of loss of trust in the company and its executives. Under the current legal system, these executives are highly unlikely to be held financially accountable, nor is it likely they will have to give back any of their incentive compensation for any short-term financial gains that they may have realized.

The reason is that under the current system, General Motors's compensation polices, like those of most corporations, permit the recovery of paid executive bonuses only in a few circumstances related to esoteric accounting. These corporate policies do not extend to situations where top executives take shortcuts or engage in other types of unethical behavior that jeopardize customers and the corporation itself.

Solution-Based Strategies

Third is the risk in the trend to more expansive customer-driven corporate strategies. More and more customers demand "solutions" rather than individual products that might not work smoothly together as an integrated system when technology and features change. An example of this trend is the irritant of modern televisions that continue to be expanded into "entertainment centers" consisting of broadcast TV, cable networks, movies available from a number of sources, and Internet access. Currently, many viewer/customers trying to negotiate through all the technologies, using multiple handheld remote controllers and wiring together multiple electronic units to access these exploding services experience severe frustration with the complexity of an activity that used to be simple.

Among a number of other corporations, Apple has been working to offer customers a seamless solution here. And as we have discussed previously, Boeing and IBM have similarly migrated to system integration strategies to attract customers. And indeed, the seamless customer experience in light of exponentially increasing technological complexity can be likened to the pursuit of the Holy Grail for twenty-first-century corporations striving for success.

The extensive outsourcing of Tier 1 components for the 787, and the resultant coordination problems, clearly illustrate the kind of risks associated with the exponentially increasing complexity. Even Boeing's inclusion of the commercial airplane pilot as an integral part of the system requires careful attention and refinement as the overall systems become ever-more complex.

While the "global standard" for pilot communications is English, the reality is that global airline pilots using English as a second language have highly varied levels of training and proficiency in practical English fluency. While Boeing's 777 has been designed and manufactured as one of the safest commercial airplanes in the world regarding systems performance and reliability, three of the rare 777 crashes have been traced to the airplane's human "pilot system."

REINVENTING THE CORPORATE BOARD
OF DIRECTORS

Reinventing the board should start with eliminating one of the most widespread sources of potential conflict of interest—that is, the practice of CEOs also serving as board chairmen. Next to come under scrutiny should be the widespread existence of excessive CEO compensation packages (and ratification by so-called independent human relations consulting firms hired by the corporations themselves). And the policies of buffering CEOs and executives from accountability for self-serving short-run strategic decisions such as damaging reductions in research and development also need to be removed.

CEO control over board agendas represents a major design flaw that can skew the corporate oversight system, as does allowing CEO influence to bias the selection of new board members. The board and its governance committee must act to ensure that the CEO's influence does not hinder the board's member make-up, nor channel information limiting the board from carrying out the fiduciary responsibilities of exercising oversight and taking action to remove CEOs who fail to provide adequate leadership for the corporation to compete effectively and remain viable.

A second critical step is eliminating the widespread persistence of weak boards incapable of overseeing CEO leadership through effective evaluation and analysis of corporate performance. The drive to assemble prestigious and diverse board members can result in boards laden with members who may be too busy or uninterested in engaging in enough effort and time to fully understand and substantively discuss corporate issues.

Perhaps even more problematic, board members are often kept in the dark about the corporation's business and challenges much more than they should be. Coupling insufficient information with an insufficient base level understanding of the corporation's strategy, financial health, compensation systems, governance, strategic role of IT, and the way that all of these interact, the board can fast become impaired in its fiduciary responsibilities to the shareholders and other stakeholders (e.g., employees, customers, and the community).

The polite, collegial failure to eliminate nonperforming board members, allowing the hangers-on to simply persist, is unsustainable. Instead, effective corporate leaders need to implement a process similar to those at professional sports teams, including continuous assessment and improvement of the board members' performance as a smoothly functioning oversight team. Directors who do not or cannot perform should be cut from the team, and more capable and motivated team members recruited and groomed to replace them.

Harvard Business School Professor Robert Pozen has made an argument for professional boards of directors to obtain the director engagement required for effective twenty-first-century corporation oversight.[24] Pozen argues for smaller boards (around seven members) with deeper subject matter experience regarding the corporation's products and processes, as well as deeper expertise in the main areas of oversight of accounting and finance, compensation, governance, and IT.[25]

Professional board candidates would have or develop the level of expertise that we now expect of directors serving on audit committees: certified accounting expertise. In essence, boards of public corporations now must certify that the chairperson of the board-level audit committee has enough knowledge and experience in accounting matters to work with the company's accounting staff and public auditor team in support of the board's oversight duties. The corporation's public auditor partner reports to the audit chair, and the audit chair and committee recommend to the board of directors the annual hiring of an audit firm to conduct the annual audit and the "fairness" opinion of the corporation's financial statements. All board members are required to read, understand, and approve the corporation's financial statements and SEC filings.

The requirement for accounting expertise could be extended to compensation expertise, governance expertise, and IT expertise. All members of twenty-first-century boards of directors should be required to obtain and maintain their expertise in these areas necessary for effective oversight. A growing number of postgraduate programs offer sitting directors education in all of these subject areas. With these developments, serving on boards of directors would be viewed similar to a profession, with its own professional code of ethics and certification criteria.[26]

The Governance Committee needs to be shored up so that it can rigorously monitor the board's team performance and the directors' individual contributions. It must act to ensure the overall effective board-level oversight of executive leadership and corporate performance.

In the twenty-first century, people are living longer, and there is a growing pool of previous CEOs, CFOs, COOs, CTO/CIOs, and public accounting partners to draw upon for twenty-first-century boards of directors. Both retired Boeing CEOs and legendary Boeing engineers effectively served on Boeing's boards of directors for years. The contributions of these Boeing board members with deep subject matter understanding and experience outweighed any concerns that these directors might inhibit the leadership of the then-serving Boeing CEOs in achieving and maintaining Boeing's industry leadership.

In other parts of the corporation, the shift to the twenty-first century requires the continued substitution of IT-enabled automation for routine, low-level company tasks. As these tasks have been replaced, workers have moved up into higher-level blue-collar work and more technical work. Accordingly, the sharp twentieth-century distinction between high-level blue-collar and white-collar work has blurred into the overall category of knowledge work—that is, work that is less defined by routine and more characterized by accumulated knowledge, experience, and innovation.

This kind of shift is visible in the work that is taking place among teams of line workers, manufacturing engineers, and design engineers as they collaborate on continuous improvements to Boeing's moving assembly lines, such as the 737 moving line at the Boeing Renton plant. Board members need to make similar shifts in the skill sets and collaborative capabilities they bring to their task.

It is instructive to reflect on the twentieth-century process of promotion from within and the pathway a number of these people steeped in the culture of the company created as board members. Boeing and Nordstrom had followed this practice providing an important continuity and wisdom to their board of directors' deliberations. Examples at Boeing include CEOs Clairmont Egtvedt, Bill Allen, and T Wilson; Bruce Nordstrom is an example at Nordstrom.

I went to the University of Washington with Jim Nordstrom, and he worked, as did his uncle, Bruce, like all entry-level employees at Nordstrom do today, putting shoes on customers' feet at the Nordstrom shoe department. Jim continued to be promoted within Nordstrom until he reached the position of president and member of the board. Along the way, he thoroughly learned the operations of the company and the company culture that was so essential to the success of the corporation. In a similar manner, Boeing recruited both factory workers and engineers that started from the bottom and worked their way up.

Although these are only two examples of promotion within and eventual board membership, it is obvious that this practice provides a very deep understanding of the subject matter of the corporation, as well as the explicit and implicit elements of the company culture that underlie the competitive success of the corporation. This kind of practice and experience is likely to be important to board oversight in strategy and execution. It follows that twenty-first-century boards should also consider tapping the company's internally developed talent in its endeavors to provide deep corporate understanding and effective corporate oversight.

Dartmouth Tuck School Professor Bob Howell advocates moving away from one-size-fits-all standardized board committees consisting of audit, compensation, and governance committees. First, Howell suggests that the full board should act as the corporation's long-term strategy standing committee—not only overseeing but also "directing" the CEO and executive team. He strongly believes that board members need to be knowledgeable about the subject matter of the corporation's business and industry and persistently discuss and direct the executive management team on competitive "fit" in the corporation's markets and industry.

Secondly, Howell advocates that beyond the three standard board committees, other board-level committees should be established based upon need and strategic importance. These board-level committees would be tailored to strategic activities and timing and disbanded upon discharge of their functions.[27]

Wayne Fisher, an active board member in the financial services industry, argues that the global environment of the twenty-first century requires boards of directors to actively address risk management to identify threats to the corporation's operations, to analyze the risks, and to undertake appropriate risk abatement programs. Fisher contends that the global scope of twenty-first-century corporations has vastly increased exposure to risks, and this exposure requires the board to provide the necessary oversight to ensure appropriate risk mitigating programs are in place.[28] A more formal risk assessment along with prior contingency planning of risk abatement programs for the 787 airplane program might have reduced surprises and costly delivery delays.

When all twenty-first-century board members are capable of understanding and providing effective oversight for accounting and finance, compensation, governance, and IT, it would make sense for committee chairs to be rotated though the board every three to five years. The nonexecutive board chairmanship could be rotated every three to five years as well. This would facilitate collaborative leadership of the board, and deeper understanding of the corporation as well as providing more informed board-level corporate performance oversight.

The acceleration of real-time information transparency—increasingly available to everyone through the Internet and smartphones—continues to expose ineffective board oversight of corporations. As an example, the Dodd-Frank legislation requires public corporations to publish the ratio between the CEO's compensation and the median pay within the company. Ratios of over a 100 to 1 are prima facie evidence of an imbalance in corporate compensation, and information transparency makes that evidence easily accessible both within and outside the organization.

Accordingly, now is the time for boards to reexamine the effectiveness of their oversight and take any and all appropriate actions that their self-assessment reveals as necessary. Taking action starts with a vision of what your twenty-first-century board should be, and then formulating a strategy for realizing it. The execution of the board strategy will require bold and difficult action. But it will be much better if the board takes proactive action rather than to have actions forced on it by legislators or courts.

TURMOIL AT THE TOP: THE REINVENTED
BOARD MUST KEEP A STEADY HAND

As often happens, real-life events intervened in the Boeing 787 program, causing it not to turn out as planned. With the sudden departure of CEO Phil Condit, the senior management team lost the top-down vision of the 787 program as a manageable product-driven transformation of the Boeing Corporation, while the team turned to coping with their defense business problems and their 787 execution problems. It seemed that the senior management team became overwhelmed and fatigued by organizational changes. The original transformative vision of propagating the learnings and new organizational structures of the 787 program to spearhead the transformation of the rest of the company was pushed into the background and then faded away. Board oversight on this issue seemingly was not forthcoming.

There remain serious flaws in the structure, membership, and capabilities among boards of directors that have limited the effective oversight of corporate performance. The flaws have increasingly allowed problems to persist, frequently negatively impacting the performance of major corporate programs, and, in turn, the performance of the overall corporation. The flaws have been widely publicized and have been increasingly criticized, resulting in a trend of greater governmental regulation. However, greater governmental regulation is insufficient. What is called for is for boards of directors to become proactive and reinvent themselves.

NOTES

1. The 2000 Boeing outside directors: Paul Gray, John McDonnell, John Shalikashvili, John Biggs, Kenneth Duberstein, John Ferry, Charles Pigott, Lewis Platt and Rozanne Ridgway.
2. Interestingly, in the early part of the twenty-first century, there seems to be an increasing number of CEOs coming to the CEO position after serving on the corporation's board of directors.
3. The 2014 board consisted of eleven members, and John McDonnell had left the board. Members of the 2014 board: Linda Z. Cook, Director since 2003, former Executive Director, Royal Dutch Shell. Kenneth M. Duberstein, Director since 1997, Chairman and CEO, The Duberstein (Consulting) Group; former White House Chief of Staff. Admiral Edumund P. Giambastiani, Jr., Director since 2009, seventh Vice Chairman of the U.S. Joint Chiefs of Staff. Lawrence W. Kellner, Director since 2011, President, Emerald Creek Group; former Chairman and CEO, Continental Airlines; Officer and Executive Director, Nielsen Holdings. Edward M. Liddy, Director since 2010, Partner, Clayton, Dubilier & Rice; former Chairman and CEO, Allstate. W. James McNerney, Jr., Director since 2001, Chairman, President, and CEO, Boeing. Mr. McNerney has served as Chairman, President, and CEO of the Boeing Company since July 2005. Previously, he served as Chairman and CEO of 3M Company (diversified technology) from January 2001 to June 2005. Beginning in 1982, he served in management positions at General Electric Company. Susan C. Schwab, Director since 2010, Professor, University of Maryland School of Public Policy; former U.S. Trade Representative. Ronald A. Williams, Director since 2010, former Chairman and CEO, Aetna. Michael S. Zalfirovski, Director since 2004, Executive Advisor, The Blackstone Group; President, The Zaf Group; former President and CEO, Nortel.
4. John McDonnell received his engineering degree at Princeton and began his career at McDonnell Aircraft as a strength engineer. He went on to executive positions at McDonnell-Douglas including CEO of the McDonnell finance division.
5. *The New York Times*, "Sunday Business," July 3, 2010, pp. 1, 5. As reported in the national index of the U.S. Social Security, the average worker annual compensation in 2007 was $40,405; in 2008 it was $41,334; and in 2009 it was $40,711; www.ssa.gov, accessed by author on December 8, 2012.
6. In 1976, Warner Bros. released their Hollywood movie: *Brinks: The Great Robbery*.

7. Healy, Paul M., and Palepu, Krishna G., "The Fall of Enron," HBS No. 109–039 (Boston: Harvard Business School Publishing, 2008). The case examines the company's dramatic fall including the extension of its trading model into questionable new businesses, the financial reporting problems, and governance breakdowns inside and outside the firm. Enron's board and management failures were among the main issues that gave rise to the Sarbanes-Oxley legislation.
8. It should be noted that during this time U.S. citizens were also raging against certain senate and congressional members for cases of alleged conflict of interests in what appeared to be unduly favorable financial arrangement with corporations through various corporate sponsored lobbying groups.
9. Senator Paul Sarbanes and Representative Michael Oxley drafted the Sarbanes-Oxley Act of 2002 to protect investors by improving the accuracy and reliability of corporate disclosures The Sarbanes-Oxley Act created new standards for corporate accountability and penalties for acts of wrongdoing. It impacts how corporate boards and executives interact with each other and with auditors. It removes the defense of "I wasn't aware of financial issues" from CEOs and CFOs, holding them accountable for the accuracy of financial statements. The Act specifies new financial reporting responsibilities for adherence to new internal controls and procedures. The Act requires all financial reports to include an internal control report designed to show that not only are the company's financial data accurate but the company also has confidence in adequate controls in place to safeguard financial data.
10. There is concern that the U.S. Congress has been impacted by problems of excesses similar to corporate executives. This opens up criticisms of congressional members in the form of "do what I say, not what I do." See Jacob S. Hacker and Paul Pierson, *Winner-Take-All Politics* (New York: Simon & Shuster, 2010).
11. On July 31, 2009, H.R. 3269, the "Corporate and Financial Institution Compensation Fairness Act of 2009" passed the House of Representatives. The House bill included a section that allowed for a "say on pay" for all public institutions in the United States. Additionally, it had a provision for a shareholder vote on golden parachutes. In the Senate, Senator Charles Schumer introduced the Shareholder Bill of Rights. The House and Senate bills were reconciled in a final bill that was signed by President Obama on July 21, 2010, called The Dodd-Frank Wall Street Reform and Consumer Protection Act.
12. At the time, this was the largest combined commercial airplane order ever received by Boeing.
13. SPEEA is the Society for Professional Engineering Employees Association.
14. Professor Michael Jensen (with William Meckling, previously at the Simon School, University of Rochester) wrote an influential paper on the subject entitled "Theory of the Firm: Managerial Behavior, Agency Costs and Ownership Structure," *Journal of Financial Economics* (1976), 1–77.
15. When Professor Jensen would remind the executives that the corporation paid the fees of the outside compensation committees, I remember their responses as not considering this to be particularly important, or that the CEO had sway over the board make-up or board agenda.
16. Bazerman, Max H., and Tenbrunsel, Ann E., *Blind Spots: Why We Fail to Do What's Right and What to Do about It* (Princeton, New Jersey: Princeton University Press, 2011).
17. It is worthy of note that similarly dubious practices that proffer special insider trading immunities for U.S. congressmen have recently come under attack. Many members of Congress come into their elected offices with a few hundred thousand dollars of personal wealth and leave as multimillionaires.

18. Bazerman, Max H., and Tenbrunsel, Ann E., "Stumbling into Bad Behavior," *The New York Times*, April 20, 2011.
19. Morgenson, Gretchen, and Story, Louise, "Naming Culprits in the Financial Crisis," *The New York Times*, April 13, 2011.
20. IT leadership continues to be unsettled and an important area for academic research. See Nolan, R. L., "Plight of the EDP Manager," *Harvard Business Review* 51, no. 3 (May–June 1973), 143–152; Nolan, R. L., "Business Needs a New Breed of EDP Manager," *Harvard Business Review* (March–April 1976), 123–133; and Austin, R. D, Nolan, R. L., and O'Donnell, S., *Adventures of an IT Leader* (Boston: Harvard Business Press, 2009).
21. Nolan, Richard L. (with F. Warren McFarlan), "Information Technology and the Board of Directors," *Harvard Business Review* (October 2005), 1–10.
22. "Taming Information Technology Risk: A New Framework for Boards of Directors," www.oliverwyman.com/ow/pdf_files/OW_EN_GRC_2011_PUBL_Taming_IT_Risk.pdf, accessed by author on July 2, 2011. This is a copy of the report.
23. Austin, Robert, O'Donnell, Shannon, and Nolan, Richard L., *Adventures of an IT Leader* (Boston: Harvard Business Press, 2009). See especially chapters 10 and 11. Also, see our related case on iPhone issues: Austin, Robert D., and Nolan, Richard L., "The iPhone at IVK," HBS No. 911–413 (Boston: Harvard Business School Press, 2010).
24. Pozen, Robert C., "The Case for Professional Boards," *Harvard Business Review*, 88, no. 12 (December 2010), 50–58.
25. Pisano and Shih likewise argue for increased technology knowledge and awareness for board members. Pisano and Shih, "Restoring American Competitiveness," *Harvard Business Review* (July 2009), 114–125. Professors Gary Pisano and Willy Shih argue that a board needs to have the same feel for technology as it has for finance and accounting.
26. Florida requires directors of Florida condominiums be certified to serve on condominium boards.
27. Based on the author's discussion and correspondence with Robert Howell, Professor, Tuck School of Business, Dartmouth College.
28. Based on the author's discussion and correspondence with Wayne H. Fisher, Executive Director, Enterprise Risk Management Institute International.

BIBLIOGRAPHY

Bazerman, Max H., and Tenbrunsel, Ann E., *Blind Spots: Why We Fail to Do What's Right and What to Do about It* (Princeton, NJ: Princeton University Press, 2011).
Jensen, Michael, and Meckling, William, "Theory of the Firm: Managerial Behavior, Agency Costs and Ownership Structure," *Journal of Financial Economics* (1976) 1–77.
Nolan, Richard L., "Ubiquitous IT: The Case of the Boeing 787 and Implications for Strategic IT Research," *Journal of Strategic Information Systems*, 21, (2012), 96–98.
Nolan, Richard L., and McFarlan, F. Warren, "Information Technology and the Board of Directors," *Harvard Business Review* (October 2005), 1–10.
Pisano, Gary, and Shih, Willy, "Restoring American Competitiveness," *Harvard Business Review* (July 2009), 114–125.
Pozen, Robert C., "The Case for Professional Boards," *Harvard Business Review*, 88, no. 12 (December 2010), 50–58.

10 From Industry Commons to Global Industry Ecosystems

Phil Condit and his executive team made two of the most impactful strategic decisions for the Boeing Corporation as it entered the twenty-first century. The first was related to acquiring the troubled McDonnell-Douglas Corporation. While this decision was bold and strategically sound, its execution was seriously flawed from the outset. The second strategic decision was an untimely decision to relocate Boeing's headquarters out of the Puget Sound industry commons to the city of Chicago. This decision physically distanced the top executive leadership by 2,000 miles from the dynamics of transforming the Boeing Corporation into a viable twenty-first-century industry leader. The suddenness of this decision and its implementation disrupted an institutionalized culture in which Boeing executives had worked and physically interacted with Boeing engineers and management on critically complex aerospace programs. These interactions had been important for keeping the executives closely informed about what was going on, as well as expediently resolving key program issues.

The relocation was followed by a controversial decision to build the second 787 final assembly line in South Carolina—3,000 miles distant from the Everett, Washington, 787 final assembly line. This decision involved recruiting and training a new non-union factory crew to staff the new assembly site. Working out the learning curve problems of this decision had an inevitable impact on the essential coordination required to "build to perfection" in manufacturing and assembling 787's to meet airline delivery contractual promises.

The momentum of any further product-driven corporate transformation was likely overwhelmed by these executive decisions regarding the 787 program.

A SEISMIC SHIFT IN CONVENTIONAL WISDOM AND THE BIRTH OF NEW STRATEGIC CHALLENGES

Twentieth-century conventional knowledge has been turned on its head. Consider Table 10.1 on size (revenue and number of employees) and market value of the largest revenue company (ExxonMobil) in the world and the

Table 10.1   Revenue and Market Value of Industry-Leading Corporations

Corporation	2012 Revenue	Number of Employees	2013 Market Value	Revenue Per Employee
Apple	$152 billion	72,800	$508 billion	$2,000,000
IBM	$104 billion	434,000	$201 billion	$240,000
Microsoft	$70 billion	94,300	$312 billion	$742,000
ExxonMobil	$482 billion	99,100	$440 billion	$486,000
Boeing	$82 billion	173,000	$104 billion	$474,000

most valuable company in the world (Apple), along with two of the most valuable companies in the computer industry (IBM and Microsoft).

Of course many factors account for the various values of these numbers for the different companies. Having said that, it is clear that total revenue has become a poor surrogate for the overall value of a company. The table also shows that the two computer industry corporations founded later in the twentieth century have the highest revenue per employee and a greater degree of virtually integrated structures than the three corporations founded nearly or more than one hundred years ago: IBM, ExxonMobil, and Boeing. It is simply much easier to flourish in the twenty-first century unencumbered by an owned vertically integrated structure. Virtually integrated industry structures provide similar benefits to owned vertically integrated structures, but without all the associated management problems and the financial drag of ownership.

Nevertheless, there is no free lunch here; as amply illustrated in the Boeing case, virtually integrated extended organizations bring their own kinds of management challenges. The Boeing and IBM transformations from highly decentralized vertically integrated organization structures to virtually integrated global organizational structures illustrate the extremely difficult management leadership challenges of any major corporate transformation.

INDUSTRY ECOSYSTEMS: A BETTER WAY TO THINK ABOUT INDUSTRY STRUCTURES, LEADERSHIP, AND THE ROLES OF MODERN CORPORATIONS WITHIN INDUSTRIES

The concept of industry ecosystems grew out of the development of the high-tech computer industry. In the computer industry, the core resources are not materials but rather systematically related ideas. The concept of modular architecture in the IBM/360 System computer became the basis of the early form of the IT industry structure. The modular architecture with simplified interfaces that buffered complexities on either side of the interface enabled the building of a powerful computer system that supported changes or complexities in either of the interacting elements without affecting the other. In addition, once built, the computer modules could be interchanged and extended if one understood the interfaces.

The IBM/360 architecture of modules and interfaces spawned the many companies making up the computer industry as we know it today. Among the companies in the industry, there is a huge amount of collaboration and fierce competition among ideas. Steve Jobs's genius was not so much in constructing hardware and software, but in envisioning new and compelling ideas about customer experiences based on the technology whereby all modules continued to smoothly work together—an early idea that became publicized with the Apple Macintosh: "works right out of the box."

Ideas are what attract contributors to the ecosystem to make the ideas a reality, and this reality in turn attracts customers to the ecosystem to make the ideas an economic success. Bold ideas are especially attractive in drawing together the essential team of talented creators to sustain high levels of innovation.

In the 1980s, the idea of "open systems" energized the computer industry ecosystem to counter IBM's proprietary power to restrict the free flow of ideas and invention into a smoothly operating ecosystem. Digital Equipment Corporation and Hewlett-Packard were also major players at the time with their own proprietary operating systems (OS).

But then AT&T bucked the trend and joined forces with Sun Micro to provide interoperable hardware on a nonproprietary operating system. The idea drew in programmers from around the world in what became the "Open Systems" movement. The Open Systems movement developed a UNIX derivative OS called Linux, whereby software programmers around the world contributed, and made available their collective work free for others to use and build on through the Internet.

In concept, this architecture was similar to the architecture of the 787 with respect to large-scale systems integration of modules including Tier 1 major components, requiring well-defined interfaces between the modules.

PLACE MATTERS

Pisano and Shih apply the concept of the town common, where farmers' animals came to graze together on the common green in colonial towns, to places of major industrial concentrations like the Puget Sound region.

An industry commons often begins with an entrepreneurial visionary like Bill Boeing. Bill Boeing understood that he could not realize his vision alone. He needed a source of trained aeronautical engineers. He went to the University of Washington and met with the Engineering Department

Chair, Professor Moore. He pitched a proposition to Moore: if you create an Aeronautical Engineering Program, I will build a wind tunnel at the University of Washington for aeronautical research. It turned out to be one of the most impactful partnerships ever, and the first two graduates of Moore's program went on to become successor CEOs to Bill Boeing. The partnership also accounted for much of the research that resulted in the game-changing Boeing 247 and 707.

The workings of any industry commons encompass a complex networking phenomenon. The mapping of the commons defies precision. The best that can be done is to map the key elements and characterize the network interactions.

Applying this approach, I have defined two time periods: 1900–1950, the formation and development of the Puget Sound region commons, and 1950–2010, the transition of the commons from a twentieth-century manufacturing-based commons to a high-tech-based commons, in which manufacturing morphed into twenty-first-century high-tech methods too. These two time periods correspond to the transition of the economy from a twentieth-century industrial economy to a twenty-first-century information economy.

In this approach, I also delineate three groups making up the commons: a core, an outer core, and a service base. The members of the commons are primarily companies, but it also includes key nonprofit organizations and nonwork organizations where people in the commons spend time networking. These interactions provide an important venue for creating relationships, establishing trust, and effectively communicating tacit knowledge as well as diverse ideas that underpin innovation processes.

Formation and Development of the Puget Sound Region Industry Commons (1900–1950)

During the first half of the twentieth century, the Puget Sound industry commons was founded on the cooperation between Boeing and the University of Washington. Boeing dominated the economic landscape of Seattle with its vertically integrated organizational structure encompassing airplane research, development and design, fabrication, manufacturing, certification, and sales. Boeing's worldwide reputation drew to Seattle an exceptional aerospace workforce. The University of Washington benefitted immensely from the success of the Boeing Company, and its support for faculty research and facilities such as one of the first-ever wind tunnels, a well-equipped early computer laboratory, and a liberal financial support program for postgraduate study for Boeing employees. Boeing benefitted from its partnership with the University of Washington through its access to an educated pool of aeronautical engineers, business graduates, and aeronautical engineering research professors. Figure 10.1 is a depiction of the 1900–1950 Puget Sound region industry commons.

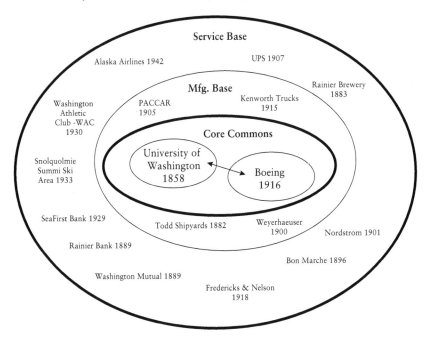

Figure 10.1 Puget Sound Region Industry Commons, 1900–1950

The Puget Sound region industry commons benefitted as Boeing and the University of Washington both drew to the region highly talented engineers and professionals—more than either could retain as full-time employees. The surplus talent generally stuck around and found employment for their unique skills in other corporations and endeavors in the Puget Sound region. More than a few founded their own start-up companies.

The manufacturing base and the service base of the commons enjoyed access to this spillover of talent, and the application of the engineering skills was soon seen in the companies in the commons. For example, both Weyerhaeuser and PACCAR became well known for their advanced engineering and use of leading computer technologies. During the hard times in the U.S. auto industry, PACCAR's commercial truck manufacturing sailed through with some of the highest return on equity (ROE) ratios in the manufacturing industry.

The commons benefitted by having a talent pool large enough to include a level of innovation and entrepreneurial interests that seeded a growing source of start-up ventures. For example, Ted Jones worked for Boeing as a supervisor, gaining valuable aerodynamic experience on the Boeing 314 Clipper—the "flying boat." Applying marine engineering knowledge that he gained at Boeing, he created the sponsons on Stan Sayre's

Slo-mo-shun III, which launched his hydroplane design business. Ted Jones designed the revolutionary *Slo-mo-shun IV*, which literally flew over the water, and *Slo-mo-shun V*. With his revolutionary hydroplane design, he and his son became the leading unlimited[1] hydroplane designers over the next three decades.

Formation and Development of the IT-Based Puget Sound Region High-Tech Industry Commons (1950–2010)

During the second half of the twentieth century and into the beginning of the twenty-first century, the Puget Sound region industry commons matured and transitioned into an IT-based high-tech commons. Most importantly, Seattle native Bill Gates returned to town, bringing with him his fledgling Microsoft Company. Microsoft grew and became a core commons organization equal to Boeing and the University of Washington. With its new structure focusing on PC operating systems and operating within the virtually integrated personal computer industry segment (see Figures 6.1 and 6.2), Microsoft rocketed by its traditionally vertically integrated rival, IBM, to become the most valuable corporation in the industry. Figure 10.2 depicts the expansion of the Puget Sound region into a high-tech industry commons.

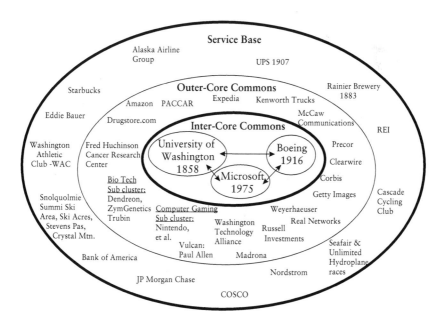

Figure 10.2   Puget Sound Region High-Tech Industry Commons, 1950–2010

PHYSICAL PLACE AND ECONOMIC CLUSTERS

Harvard Business School Professor Michael Porter researched places like the Puget Sound region and characterized them as economic "clusters." Porter defined clusters as geographic concentrations of interconnected companies and institutions in a particular field. He argued the importance of clusters in the new economics of competition.[2] Porter extended his research by establishing the Cluster Mapping Project at the Institute for Strategy and Competitiveness at Harvard University. The project collected and made available both economic performance and innovation output statistics for U.S. economic clusters. The statistics for the "Seattle-Tacoma-Bellevue, Washington Metropolitan Area Economic Performance Indicators for 2008" include:[3]

- Employment: Total 2008 private, nonagricultural employment in Seattle-Tacoma, Washington, was 1,574,686, which was 1.3 percent of national employment.
- Employment Growth: Employment growth per year from 1998–2008 in Seattle-Tacoma, Washington, was 1.56 percent versus 1.12 percent for the United States, or 21.61 percent above the national average.
- Patents: There were eighteen patents per 10,000 employees in Seattle-Tacoma, Washington, versus 6.24 for the United States.
- Patent Growth: Patenting growth per year from 1998–2008 in Seattle-Tacoma, Washington, was 8.2 percent versus 0.47 percent for the United States.

Table 10.2 shows data from the Cluster Mapping Project for eight companies in the Seattle-Tacoma-Bellevue, Washington Metropolitan Area, that recorded more than one hundred patents each between 2004 and 2008.

The Cluster Mapping Project data revealed the workings of an industry commons in creating both increased economic activity and high levels of innovation. Like many industry commons, the happenstance of its origin

Table 10.2   Patent Activity by Major Puget Sound Region Companies

Rank	Company/Institution	Total Patents 2004–2008
1	Microsoft Corporation	5,943
2	Boeing Company	932
3	Intel	263
4	University of Washington	159
5	Honeywell International. Inc	136
6	Zymogenetics	135
7	Cypress Semiconductor, Inc.	121
8	Weyerhaeuser Company	109

is often historical accident along with other factors that come together to strengthen and broaden the industry commons.

University/company relationships have many important dimensions in a strong industry commons. Research and a steady stream of trained human resources is one of the most important, and this is often referred to as the "seed corn" of the industry commons.[4] Over time, the University of Washington created leading academic programs in aerospace engineering, computer science, and medical science that continued to attract talented students from around the world. In addition, a virtual cycle drew into the industry commons other organizations that wanted closer relationships with the anchor industry commons companies such as Nintendo and Google. The large numbers of talented people along with high levels of innovation led to a healthy stream of start-ups and new ventures, spanning variations of the industry commons' core technologies as well as extension of the core technologies.

As we can see from the Table 10.1 data from the Cluster Mapping Project, both Intel and Honeywell established major operations in the Puget Sound region industry commons, and more recently, so did Google. Also, a number of start-up companies emerged in the biotech field from research on the mapping of the genome. The University of Washington became a major research university in the biotech field. In fact, the University of Washington reached parity with Johns Hopkins University in attracting health sciences research grants and in MIT in federal science research grants.

THE INDUSTRY COMMONS: PHYSICAL PLACE MATTERS

Knowledge can't be told. Knowledge is intrinsically embedded in people among a complex set of organizations—companies, universities, think-tanks, industry associations, and nonwork places like cycling clubs, ski slopes, and recreational/social clubs (e.g., the downtown Seattle Washington Athletic Club—operating since 1930). And knowledge sharing is dependent on a large number of factors such as trust, relationships, and a sharing of concepts and frameworks from various disciplines. Human processes of communication that go beyond the written and vocal characterize the process of tacit knowledge sharing. It's not easy to capture the many dimensions that make knowledge sharing and collaboration so essential to a healthy industry commons. A few examples and illustrations taken from the unique nature of the Puget Sound region industry commons help to illustrate the breadth and intricacies of the process.

The Recreational Dimension

Recreational activities are an important dimension in bringing people together and facilitating communications about shared interests. In the

Puget Sound region, these activities facilitate Boeing engineers learning from University of Washington professors—and vice versa. Proximity and shared interests facilitate PACCAR workers learning from Microsoft workers on the use of IT technology to create value in their commercial trucks. Likewise Nordstrom IT people learn from Microsoft employees about computer-based supply chain management; and Microsoft learns from Nordstrom and Starbucks about outstanding customer service, the lifetime value of a customer relationship, and the concept of creating value in their customers' experiences. Virginia Mason Hospital learned of Boeing's lean manufacturing 737 moving line that had reduced 737 construction from twenty-two days to eleven days. The hospital's CEO, Dr. Gary Kaplan, and his team visited with Boeing managers and other lean manufacturing sites to learn how they might apply similar concepts in hospitals. From 2002–2010 Virginia Mason Hospital implemented lean manufacturing techniques.[5] Kaplan and his team went on to win the John Eisenberg Patient Safety Award and Quality Award given by the National Quality Forum and Joint Commission.

These interactions and relationships take place in many venues in the Puget Sound region. Many take place on the slopes of the ski areas on Mount Rainier, the Cascades, and the Olympics—all within a day's drive from Seattle, with parents and ski buses taking the kids of Seattle up to the slopes to learn to ski and snowboard at early ages. People with similar interests come together and create places where interactions transpire—such as the ski lodge at Stevens Pass initially established by Boeing workers, but selectively open to other invited guests.

After we worked together on the Boeing/UW AIMS ExecEd program for more than a couple of years, a Boeing manager who was an expert skier and a longtime member of the Stevens Pass lodge invited me to ski with the group. The invitation transpired after he had sort of qualified me to ski and informally meet and discuss ideas within the context of shared interests among this group. While this group originated as a Boeing group, its members had expanded through the years to encompass a diverse group of managers, academics, and others in the Puget Sound high-tech commons.

The inner core of the Puget Sound high-tech commons operates like the fertile "soup" of the commons creating a virtuous circle of nurturing ideas and innovation. The virtuous circle ideas and innovations then are brought back to the organizations where the people work, and many are adopted in some form. Diverse corporations like Nordstrom, Amazon, and Starbucks have benefited by adapting wide-ranging ideas and innovations into their unique operations.

This process, in turn, continues to attract leading corporations in their respective industries like Google and Getty Systems to locate in the commons and became integral parts of the industry commons.

THE VIRTUAL PLACE OF THE PUGET SOUND INDUSTRY COMMONS

Another important lesson to be learned is that today's industry commons are beginning to extend beyond the physical place of the commons to a geographically widespread virtual commons, largely made possible by modern IT. The phenomenon spreads and extends the common synergies. For example, Microsoft established a large research activity in China strengthened by both physical and virtual collaboration among Microsoft's software engineers. Boeing's global outsourcing creates links to a wide variety of aerospace strategic partners and people that can be tightened into purposeful networks to work on common problems.

Starting with Phil Condit's efforts working in Italy to jointly design a small commercial jet, Boeing has continued to expand its global reach and partnering activities. While the effort in Italy did not result in the joint development of a new commercial jet, it did create a long-term parts manufacturing relationship; the relationship then evolved into building the more complex Tier 1 components for the 787. As the global sale figures for commercial airplanes have grown, so have important "off-set" partnerships expanded as Boeing has continued to establish a global outsourcing network, and an extended global supply chain network.

There is a lot of important learning that is going on as twenty-first-century corporations continue to learn the importance of "place"—both physical and virtual. Boeing and its global strategic partners were breaking new ground in enabling Boeing to focus on its core capabilities in large systems integration, and tap into the global workforce for comparative advantages in talent and cost structures in both designing and manufacturing the 787.

The strategy was bold. Learning to operate in the virtual commons involved new concepts such as extending the corporate culture into the virtual space; forging trust with strategic partners; and learning how to manage partner relationships by creating, maintaining, tightening, and loosening relationships as needed. As it turned out, these challenges stretched the execution and change capacity of the in-place Boeing management team. This was in spite of the elaborate IT infrastructure put in place, consisting of a common CAD/CAM system to coordinate design, and a global state-of-the-art high-speed data communication and video conferencing facility that operated 24/7 during the entire year. And indeed, the IT infrastructure did work to an extent, but not enough to solidify the outsourcer relationships and build the trust among the global participants to effectively manage the network and avoid the extended supply chain problems that developed.

Many of Boeing's problems with coordination and the global supply chain can be traced to making the virtual place an effective extension of the physical place. Here there were myriad of issues involving tacit knowledge communication, relationship, culture, and trust. Effectively coping with these challenges remains in an early state of learning and development for most global corporations.

Some of the issues began with the charade of rolling out the jury-rigged first 787 as the TV cameras rolled, in an attempt to mislead airline customers and others into thinking that the 787 program was on track and that deliveries would be made as scheduled. The senior management had ample information that deliveries would be significantly delayed. Trust among customers was damaged, and the Boeing rank and file began to question their confidence in the senior management leadership.

The sudden move of the Boeing headquarters from Seattle to Chicago physically isolated the corporate executive team from its culture of frequent "walk-arounds" in maintaining a sense of what was going on in the execution of commercial airplane programs, as well as engaging in the on-site collaboration of the executive teams in executing their strategies.

The supply chain shortage of fasteners due to outsourcing partners' hoarding was not discovered until it had become a serious problem translating to delivery delays. The supply chain IT systems were not extended down to lower-tier partners to reveal the problem in a timely manner. The failure to identify hoarding patterns may have indicated a lack of trust among the 787 partners and Boeing.

The continued problems with the extended network of outsourcing partners caused Boeing to partially depart from the bold strategic partner approach and scramble to gain control of the manufacturing process by acquiring some outsourced manufacturing facilities and deploying Boeing employees to outsourcer sites. Further confusion resulted. After billions of dollars of unexpected expenses, the issues with trust and working relationships between outsourcer partners and the Boeing workers became intractable. Repairing them would take years, rather than weeks or months. This was the cost of cumulative mistakes attributable to the Boeing executive team and weak board oversight.

Boeing's problems here are not unique. It has taken many years for the architecture of open systems to be assimilated into the computer industry, and there still remain issues in the industry. Particularly, the traditional corporations in the industry such as IBM and Microsoft fought the movement before learning to live within the new industry architecture and ecosystem. A similar process is taking place in the aerospace industry, and the Boeing Corporation got out on the leading edge of the industry restructuring with their 787 program. Important issues began with the definition and design of the 787 modules and their interfaces. This was followed by creating the processes for carrying out the work necessary to manufacture the modules and assemble them with flawless interfaces designed to "click" together smoothly into a finished commercial airplane. The failures were big and costly surprises. Any time relationships, trust, and people are involved in a radically different approach to work, it is almost always harder than originally thought. When the work spans the globe and different cultures, the challenges can become exponentially difficult, and rarely can they be resolved on the fly.

THOUGHTS ON THE FUTURE ECOSYSTEMS

Ecosystem networks are integral to the performance of twenty-first-century corporations. Given the importance of operating within a vibrant industry ecosystem, Boeing's decision to make Chicago its headquarters, leaving behind the Puget Sound high-tech industry commons ecosystem where, as an anchor corporation, the company benefitted from many important relationships, had unanticipated side effects. Chicago simply could not offer an aerospace industry ecosystems commons like the one in Puget Sound.

The twenty-first-century IT technologies have had an impact on the role of place in industry ecosystems. Physical place is important, and now so is virtual space. In the new global industry commons and ecosystems, the advantages of physical proximity for collaboration and communication of intrinsic knowledge can be extended in virtual space.

The concept of place needs to embody the idea of the corporation operating globally as its ecosystem expands, contracts, and changes as dictated by the corporation's strategy, the location of capabilities necessary to execute its strategy, and the ever-changing challenges of its competitive environment. Learning to extend the concept of the local industry ecosystem to build relationships, trust, and communications in the global industry ecosystem is a big twenty-first-century challenge for executive leadership teams. One important lesson of the Boeing 787 program is the need to fully understand this challenge and take action to meet it at the outset rather than retrospectively encountering the expensive lesson and having to spend years recovering from it.

NOTES

1. The term "unlimited" was included in the description of these racing boats to indicate that at the time no limits were made on the propulsion in type or horsepower, or in architecture design of the hull.
2. Porter, Michael E., "Clusters and the New Economics of Competition," *Harvard Business Review* (November–December 1998). Also see Porter, Michael E., *On Competition* (Boston: Harvard Business School Press, 1998).
3. Source: Professor Michael E. Porter, Cluster Mapping Project, Institute for Strategy and Competitiveness, Harvard Business School; Richard Bryden, Project Director, www.clustermapping.us, accessed by author on July 8, 2011.
4. On March 18th, I attended the 2011 Washington Innovation Summit at Microsoft sponsored by the Washington Technology Alliance—a high-technology nonprofit organization in the Puget Sound region. At the Summit, a number of the speakers commented on the importance of the University of Washington in

providing the "seed corn" for the continued health of the Puget Sound region industry commons. The speakers also commented on the importance of both Boeing and Microsoft in recruiting highly trained engineers and other human resources into the Puget Sound region to supply the talent needed for the important ventures and spinoffs in the Puget Sound region industry commons.

5. Bohmer, Richard M. J., and Ferlins, Erika M., "Virginia Mason Medical Center," HBS case 9–606–044, Revised October 3, 2008.

BIBLIOGRAPHY

Pisano, Gary P., and Shih, Willy C., "Restoring American Competitiveness," *Harvard Business Review*, 87, nos. 7–8 (July–August 2009), 2–14.

Porter, Michael E. "Clusters and the New Economics of Competition," *Harvard Business Review*, 76, no. 6 (November–December 1998), 77–90.

Porter, Michael E., *On Competition* (Boston: Harvard Business School Press, 1998).

11 The Modern Corporation in the World

Modern corporations represent tremendous economic and creative power that can be channeled to good causes, or—in too many cases—to support unbridled greed, with the negative consequences that can ensue.

Since the early 1900s, corporations have continued to extend their operations to create today's diverse global economy. More than a few modern corporations have become larger and more influential than many sovereign countries. Corporations have extended their operations with little restraint—seemingly only limited by their investment bankers' and corporate lawyers' imaginations.[1] And in the process, modern corporations have become so pervasive that world populations are more dependent on them than ever before for their food, services, technologies, work, and daily well-being.

This phenomenal growth has conferred increasing power on corporations not only in commerce but also in politics, governments, and society. This power has been highly concentrated in CEOs and their executive teams. Checks and balances from governmental regulatory processes and oversight from boards of directors have not kept pace. The gap shows up repeatedly in signs of corporate abuse—some subtle, but others more frequently have been astonishingly consequential and broader in scope.

In an earlier age, as the nineteenth century gave way to the twentieth, corporate structures already revealed dramatic signs of abuse, in particular through the formation of large railroad corporate trusts exercising unconstrained monopoly power. President Theodore Roosevelt responded to these abuses with his "trust buster" leadership and legislative initiatives.[2]

A seminal academic book published in 1932 by Adolf Berle and Gardiner Means alerted the public to the risks of separating ownership from control in the structure of the modern corporation[3]—that is, in the eyes of the common law, a public corporation will be treated as an "artificial person," with rights similar to those of humans. For example, corporations could potentially sue people for alleged persecution of their individual rights guaranteed by the U.S. Constitution. A public corporation entitled to religious beliefs allowed the corporation to deny workers of certain persuasions worker benefits. The right of free speech allowed corporations to spend large sums of money to influence the political process.

In their book, *The Modern Corporation and Private Property*, Berle and Means go on to point out that the separation of ownership from management could destroy the owner's traditional interests and motivations regarding property rights. Shareholders would be stripped of motivational power and as a result might become disinterested. Treating the corporation as an "artificial person" allowed the corporation to be sued for illegal activity but limited the shareholders' risk only to the value of their initial share investments, rather than the individual owner's potential loss of the entire company's value. In this new system, "agents" (professional managers or stewards) began to make decisions that had traditionally been the purview of owners and wielded the power of the corporation to implement them. This arrangement created a conflict between the interests and motivations of stewards, who held the power of the corporation, and the interests of corporate shareholders.

Nearly a century later, we can see many signs of the resulting dysfunction, including runaway CEO compensation and the buffering of corporate leadership from direct accountability for decisions. Too often, the personal motivations of management, or agents, are put ahead of shareholders. These effects have been exacerbated by weaker corporate boards of directors, elected by shareholders to maintain shareholder interests, but largely beholden to executive management. The problems have worsened, as corporations have grown increasingly complex and expansive.

In the 1950s another seminal academic work by Dahl and Lindblom, *Politics, Economics, and Welfare*, alerted the public about the convergence of power among public corporations and governmental and social organizations across the globe.[4] Again, this was a major academic commentary on the rise and growth of the modern corporation and the implications.

THE SHIFT TOWARD HIGHER-RISK CORPORATE STRATEGIES IN THE TWENTY-FIRST CENTURY

General Electric's strategic dictum, "Be number one or number two in your business, or sell" was remarkably influential in the late twentieth century. MBA programs, as well as executive education programs, incorporated it into their teaching about business strategy. The corollaries included popular adages such as "if you can't measure it, you can't manage it" and "a good manager can manage anything."

But this kind of received wisdom undermined the importance of substantive subject knowledge in executive leaders' understanding of the science and practical experience of the corporations' core products and services as responses to customers' needs. At the dawn of the new century, systems integration, responsiveness to customers, and ease of use had emerged as central to most corporate strategies. However, the bias toward financial stewardship remained, especially among those corporations founded in the twentieth century.

There is a clear trend of twenty-first-century global corporate strategies moving away from biased financial engineering, if not approaching a tipping point, toward broader-oriented strategies based on customer service and responsiveness. Direct customer influence is a recurring theme in these rapidly emerging strategies. There is also a strong move toward "works-out-of-the-box" or ease of use, reflecting the spirit of Steve Jobs.

The Macintosh computer worked quite quickly soon after the customer pulled it out of the box. The Apple product designers strived to get the product quickly working for its customers, without the customer first having to read thick manuals of hard-to-understand instructions. Customers found the Mac personal computers more intuitive and faster to get up and running than its competitor PCs.

We can see related benefits in Phil Condit's strategy for Boeing's commercial airplane programs, especially as customers began directly influencing the actual design and manufacturing of Boeing's commercial airplanes. To implement a customer-influenced strategy, as embedded in Boeing's 757/767 and 777 series airplane[5] programs, it required careful realignment of corporate culture and structure to fit the strategy.

Culture remains an important corporate asset requiring continuous monitoring and adjustment. Structure extends the corporation into the global economy through strategic partnerships, spanning the beginning of the supply chain all the way through to end customers during the lifecycle of the product/services. More than ever, the extended organization must build quality and reliability into the product to avoid expensive recalls because of product problems or failures.

The Boeing 757/767 Story

With the deregulation of the U.S. aviation market in 1978, the competition intensified between Boeing and Airbus. Boeing had designed both the two-engine configured 757 and 767 airplanes for nonstop service across the United States. With extra-large wings and the same powerful engines used on the four-engine Boeing 747, the 767 was designed in anticipation of trans-Atlantic service. But at the time, aviation regulators did not allow two-engine airplanes to cross the Atlantic in an optimal direct routing, instead requiring them to stay within range of the nearest airports along the way.

While the four-engine Boeing 747 (which entered service in 1970), with a passenger capacity of about four hundred had decreased the fuel requirements by 30 percent compared to the Boeing 707, the new "twins" would be able to carry two hundred passengers point to point at a similarly impressive economics of 30 percent decrease in operating costs. Accordingly, airlines were eager to fly the twins over the Atlantic and open up more cities point to point, as well as increase the frequency of flights.

After several years of work involving regulators in the United States and Europe, manufacturers, airlines, and pilot unions, the Federal Aviation

Agency (FAA) issued a final set of ETOP (extended-range twin operations) standards in 1985 allowing twins to operate up to 120 minutes from the nearest airport.

The twins performed well and the Boeing 767 quickly became the dominant choice of airlines crossing the Atlantic just as the Boeing 747 had come to dominate long-haul trans-ocean airline travel. The twin-engine planes operated so well that in 1988, regulators extended the maximum level of ETOPS to 180 minutes. Airbus responded to the Boeing 767 competition with its 330 twin-engine airplane seating up to 335 passengers.

Boeing responded in turn to consider a larger capacity 767—the 767-X. In light of Airbus's aggressive competition directly challenging Boeing's industry leadership, the Boeing team stepped back to make a comprehensive analysis of its corporate competitive health. The team started with a broad analysis of its corporate culture. Boeing's corporate culture had deep roots originating from its founder, balancing two somewhat opposing factors: technology and building to perfection—as illustrated in the following continuum:

LET NO TEHNOLOGY   BUILD TO

PASS US BY←————X————→PERFECTION

This delicate balance (designated by the X) had guided the company from the beginning, through the WWII years of the B-17, the Cold War with the B-52, and later the B-707, B-727, and B-737. The balance was reinforced in Boeing's engineering culture—which encompassed both design engineering and manufacturing engineering. It was further strengthened by promotion from within, the creation of a "Distinguished Engineer" program, and CEO Bill Allen's statement that Boeing would "build the best airplane, and our customers will buy it."

With time and the increased institutionalization of the engineering emphasis, other factors impacted the Boeing culture. During the 1970s, Boeing and corporations in general became much larger and more complex. More sophisticated management techniques and cost control techniques came to the fore. These factors evolved and established a new reality during Phil Condit's tenure. At the same time, Airbus had grown to be a fierce competitor not only by building highly competitive commercial airliners but also by aggressively undercutting the price of Boeing airliners.

Condit as chief engineer for the 757 program noted that at the time of airplane design, Boeing engineers operated without accountants on the design teams. This practice could be traced to a time when Boeing's culture maintained a strong focus on building the best and most reliable commercial airplanes possible. Rather than building total cost in during design, cost was determined after the airplane had been built—that is, cost after the fact. The engineers designed without direct information on costs. The airplane was priced after the design was completed. This often resulted in the designers' specifying very expensive parts used on Boeing airplanes when perfectly suitable alternative parts could have been used to significantly lower the total cost of the airplane.

At the same time, total lifecycle, or total ownership, cost was becoming a more prominent subject in management curricula. Condit responded by bringing accountants onto design/build teams and insisting that customers participate on design/build teams as well. Airline customers and their staff could often provide information related to in-service airplane maintenance efficiencies and economies. The result was a rebalancing of Boeing's culture in the 1990s.

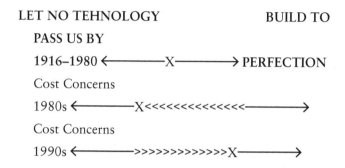

LET NO TEHNOLOGY   BUILD TO

PASS US BY

1916–1980 ←————X————→ PERFECTION

Cost Concerns

1980s ←————X<<<<<<<<<<<<<————→

Cost Concerns

1990s ←————>>>>>>>>>>>>>X————→

The Boeing 777 Story

Condit and the 757/767 team continued to assess the Airbus competition versus Boeing's competitive strengths. In 1990, the team decided to terminate the 767-X program's incremental approach and more boldly and strategically introduce an all new airplane program: the Boeing 777. The new airplane would involve two major breakthroughs. It would be completely computer-based design, forgoing the dependence on physical prototypes. And it would be ETOPs ready "out-of-the-box." In other words, Boeing would work with the airline regulators to build in the reliability for flying over the Pacific Ocean during manufacturing rather than providing the airplane to the airlines and then through flying experience demonstrate evidence for extended ETOP's certification. This would require extensive leveraging of Boeing's capabilities to build in new technologies and reliability into the airplane during "manufacturing to perfection." It also entailed structural changes to accommodate multidisciplinary "design/build" teams made up of Boeing employees as well as other stakeholders outside Boeing (e.g., customers and regulators).

Successful execution of the strategy not only saved Boeing billions of dollars, but also resulted in one of the most reliable and safest commercial airliners ever built, plus significant savings to airlines for changes and maintenance of in-service airplanes. Soon, the 777 dominated the more challenging trans-Pacific market in a similar way that the 767 dominated the trans-Atlantic market.

CREATING AND EXECUTING A SUCCESSFUL CHANGE AGENDA

Boeing's experiences with the757/767 and 777 are representative of the intricate and integrated shifts in the cultures, strategies, and structure of twenty-first-century corporations. While most corporate executives and directors understand well the need for corporate changes, few have embraced the totality of the changes, the integrated nature of the changes, and the need for a coherent and comprehensive agenda for leading and making the changes.

Since each corporation differs on factors such as size, industry, and competitive position, a one-size agenda to fit all is not realistic. The overall task can be likened to solving continuously changing multivariable simultaneous equation. It is almost impossible to keep everything in mind and solve such equations in your head. You must parse the task and create explicit agendas, accountabilities, and oversight scenarios. Several essential ingredients are important to a successful change program:

1. getting started
2. reasserting effective board leadership, control, and strategic oversight
3. establishing a twenty-first-century working agenda
4. managing oversight of the execution of the agenda

Getting Started

Getting started can be and often is the hardest part. It has to begin at the top. Many obstructions exist: weak boards, structural problems with entrenched CEOs simultaneously serving as the board chairperson, and a general lack of understanding of a critical need to change are just a few.

One transition I am familiar with started with pressure to strengthen the corporate board of directors. The first step was the appointment of a lead director. Second was separating the CEO and board chair positions, and then electing the lead director as chairman of the board. Third was a comprehensive assessment of the CEO's performance by the board, and replacement of the CEO.[6] Fourth was the assessment of the chairman of the board by the Governance Committee resulting in the election of a new chairman of the board. Fifth was inside and outside assessments of board members' performances initiated by the new board chairman and the chair of the Governance Committee. This ultimately led to restructuring the board and bringing on new board members with the needed commitment and capabilities.

The restructured board was smaller (nine members versus twelve) but stronger with respect to factors including industry expertise, executive leadership, and extended capabilities in board committee areas such as strategy, governance, accounting, and compensation. The board restructuring was done over a year: six months for assessments and restructuring, and another six months for the restructured board to build relationships and begin to work effectively together.

Reasserting Effective Board Strategic Leadership, Control, and Oversight from the Board

Leadership within this restructured board was focused on maintaining corporate shareholders' and stakeholders' best interests in the twenty-first-century competitive environment. The board was fortunate to have a board chair, who was not only a previously successful CEO in the industry and still active in the industry professional organizations but who had also gained valuable experience over the years by serving on other boards. Under the changed structure in separation of the CEO as chairman of the board, he forged a strong working relationship with the new CEO.

This relationship involved spending time with both board members and the CEO debating strategic issues and facilitating communications among the board, the CEO, and the CEO's executive team. The additional work here was recognized by the board, and the board members voted to recognize these contributions with added compensation for the chair. Although the professional contribution provided by boards of directors generally outweighs compensation considerations, the board members in this case decided that as a matter of signaling and equity, the additional compensation was important.

The board directed its compensation committee to consider the matter, which they did, and came back to the whole board with a recommendation. The recommendation was debated and voted to approve.

Depending on the corporate board's history and legacies, it can take a long time for a restructured board to learn to work together, gain effective control, and execute strategic oversight of corporate performance. A very important process here is for the board to conduct private meetings both with and without the CEO. At times, the board needs discretion and authority to consult with a diverse set of experts. In addition, the board committees need to build trust among members and create collaborative working relationships.

In chapter 9, we discussed the importance of all board members building a robust understanding of the corporation's key processes of governance, compensation, and accounting. One way to achieve this is to periodically rotate committee chairs throughout the board members. Similar to the process of learning to become a general manager, this approach would build broad subject matter expertise and create a cadre of "general board members."

The goal is to strive for an active and engaged board that retains the critical capabilities to carry out effective strategic oversight as well as the fiduciary responsibilities of board level leadership.

Establishing and Executing a Twenty-First Century Working Agenda

There are a number of prerequisites for creating an effective working agenda. First is the need to effectively communicate to the organization the need for change. As many have articulated, transformational change is facilitated by crises such as declining financial performance or a severe competitive threat. However, if the corporation is not experiencing a widely felt crisis, the executive team must define and communicate the compelling need for transformational change. People will undermine and fight changes they don't understand or they don't accept the need for.

To directly address this potential problem, a corporate story needs to be carefully developed to make a compelling argument for corporate change. The story needs to assess the current situation succinctly and present a compelling argument for the urgency of the change agenda. The argument needs to be fact based, and point to a clearly defined better state. The better state must have clearly articulated benefits that resonate with the people of the corporation.

A second prerequisite is frequently the need to address a noncompetitive corporate cost structure problem at the outset. This problem often has roots in holding on too long to an increasingly obsolete overly decentralized twentieth-century functional hierarchical organization structure. As we learned from IBM's approach in benchmarking its major costs to identify best practices, it is critical to ensure that the corporation has a competitive cost structure. The competitive cost structure enables the corporation to compete on important factors such as innovative products and high levels of customer service.

In summary, a working agenda for executing change in becoming a successful twenty-first-century corporation can be categorized into four key categories: structure, "corporate story," culture, and leadership. While restructuring the board is the first step, restructuring for cost competitiveness is the second step. Following these two structural changes, additional structural changes include adjusting the balance between stewards and creators, integrating virtual organization structures, and designing the organization to accommodate management by wire. Most likely, the newly defined future state will involve a product/service combination for the customer that "works out of the box."

The corporate culture largely determines what a corporation can execute and what it cannot execute in pursuit of the corporate strategy. Accordingly, it is important to stay attuned to the state of corporate culture and dynamically manage it from what it is to what it needs to be.

Corporate executive leadership and management must embody a number of key characteristics including:

- knowing what you don't know and engaging in team-based collaborative learning to fill the gaps
- real-time sensing and responding to customers in dynamically allocating resources

- sustaining continuous innovation by maintaining the right balance of power between stewards and creators
- nurturing a healthy industry ecosystem within both physical and virtual interactions

Sustaining Momentum/Managing Oversight of the Execution of the Agenda

Finally, success in thriving as a successful twenty-first-century corporation is critically dependent on maintaining a strong and active board to carry out active oversight of the corporate strategy, its execution, and long-term performance.

NOTES

1. A relatively recent trend, known as an "inversion" has been a legal maneuver of U.S. corporations declaring that a corporation's U.S. operations are owned by one of its foreign subsidiaries to shift reported profits out of U.S. jurisdiction to a country with a lower tax rate. Ultimately, this is a financial engineering maneuver and, similar to other financial engineering maneuvers, may have many implications including adverse effects to the corporation and its shareholders.
2. Theodore Roosevelt was the twenty-sixth president of the United States; he served from 1901 to 1909 and gained a reputation as "trust buster."
3. Berle, Adolf A., and Means, Gardiner C., *The Modern Corporation and Private Property* (New York: Macmillan, 1932).
4. Dahl, Robert A., and Lindblom, Charles E., *Politics, Economics, and Welfare* (Chicago: University of Chicago Press, 1953).
5. The Boeing 767 and 757 entered service in 1982, and Boeing 777 entered service in 1995.
6. It is important not to underestimate how tricky and difficult it is for a board to replace a sitting CEO in the current environment. I chaired the governance committee of a public corporation. Our governance committee and outside board of directors concluded that the board needed to separate the CEO and chairman of the board positions, which the governance committee and the board accomplished. The previous CEO remained Chairman of the Board. He led an initiative to decrease the size of the board, and I was asked to leave the board. Of course it is difficult to understand the motivations here, but this kind of action is not unique in similar situations.

BIBLIOGRAPHY

Berle, Adolf A., and Means, Gardiner C., *The Modern Corporation and Private Property* (New York: Macmillan, 1932).
Dahl, Robert A., and Lindblom, Charles E., *Politics, Economics, and Welfare* (Chicago: University of Chicago Press, 1953).

Epilogue

My purpose for this book was to provide the reader with perspective on the evolution of the corporation into the twenty-first century and extract what we have learned and can learn from it. Boeing's 787 Dreamliner program provided grounding for the research through the experience of one of the most important and admired corporations in the world. Using the Boeing Corporation to exemplify the overall development of the corporation during the twentieth century into the twenty-first offered vivid illustrations of the challenges in transforming a longtime industry leader to compete in the new IT-enabled environment.

Some readers may misinterpret the intent of my critical analysis of the executive team responsible for leading Boeing's 787 program. I strive not to be overcritical but rather to assess the evolution of corporations into exceedingly large, complex, global organizations faced with the opportunity to create highly innovative economic goods and services at speeds and reliabilities never before possible. To do this requires making a comprehensive baseline audit of the strengths and weaknesses of the corporation; stripping away legacies in organization structure; replacing obsolete management practices; and retooling leadership and oversight processes to cope with real-time, dynamic sense-and-respond resource allocation and decision making.

My hope is for the lessons drawn from my case research to be useful guidelines for corporate leaders as they build the capabilities to achieve the full potential of the twenty-first-century organization. In summary, these lessons include:

- Get the corporate vision and strategy "right" and clearly communicate the story.
- Ensure leadership understanding of what the corporate culture is, what it should be, and how to use consistent culture messaging to lead the necessary change.
- Embrace and implement real-time "sense-and-respond" execution including dynamic resource allocation.
- Restructure the corporate organization to embrace IT-enabled "management by wire."

- Maintain balance between creators and stewards for sustained innovation.
- Strategically manage information as a resource.
- Reinvent the corporate board of directors to provide informed oversight of corporate leadership, strategy, and execution.

Finally, I hope that all of us will recognize that the modern corporation has reached levels of complexity and importance that surpass the traditional realm of CEO and board leadership. In this case, the world isn't like it has always has been. The execution of transformational programs like the Dreamliner will continue to challenge CEO and board leadership like nothing before. These programs are a call to action for a different kind of corporation led by a different kind of executive team and board.

I have long watched the Boeing Corporation, and I maintain admiration for what Boeing has accomplished, the quality of its leadership, the depth of its culture, and, most importantly, its resilience in tackling the challenges that have confronted it. Boeing has prevailed for more than ninety years, and I suspect will resolve the challenges of its Dreamliner program in time to celebrate its one hundredth anniversary in 2016.

About the Author and Research

I grew up on Seattle's Beacon Hill overlooking Boeing Field. My childhood memories included the roar of jet engines drowning out playtime chatter, and apocryphal rumors of Boeing workers walking too close to the roaring jet engines, getting sucked in and spit out in little pieces. Some years later, standing on the shores of Lake Washington during the 1955 Gold Cup hydroplane races, I and thousands of spectators were startled to see a sleek four-jet engine Boeing 707 barrel roll over the race course not just once, but twice.[1] In many ways, this event marked the beginning of the jet age and the path of Boeing to industry leadership. Like so many people before me, I wanted to be a part of this bold and innovative company.

After graduating from the University of Washington with my doctorate in 1966, I got my wish. My Boeing job started with three months of training on programming the Univac 1108 and the IBM 360/50 Boeing computers, and then applying simulation modeling on a Minuteman project in the aerospace division. Shortly thereafter, Boeing re-shifted its focus to commercial airplane manufacturing by establishing branches for its main commercial airplane products: the 707, 727, and the 737.

I was assigned as financial systems manager for the 737 Branch. The 737 is still manufactured today, and more 737's have been sold than any other commercial airplane in history.

On April 9, 1967, as a manager, I witnessed the maiden flight of the 737. I heard one observer say, "Think of it, one million parts all flying in close formation near the speed of sound!" Little did I realize I was working for a high-tech company that was on its way to 37 years of industry dominance.

Newly married, Pam and I left Seattle and Boeing, where I began my academic career at the University of Illinois. I later joined the McNamara "whiz kid" group at the Pentagon, overseeing development of the giant C-5A military cargo airplane. In 1969, I accepted a faculty position at the Harvard Business School (HBS). After eight years on the HBS faculty developing a stages theory of information technology growth in companies, I left with a colleague, and co-founded a strategic IT consulting company: Nolan, Norton and Company. We built our company into a leader in our industry, and after 14 years merged it into KPMG Peat Marwick. I returned to the HBS faculty as the endowed William Barclay Harding Professor[2] to continue my study of CEO leadership and business transformation.

During the next 13 years, I researched and developed HBS cases on the rapid growth of high-tech companies (e.g., Cisco Systems), and business transformation (e.g., the IBM turnaround). These cases provided the background for my books on business transformation, including my HBS Press book co-authored with David Croson: *Creative Destruction*, and a book on the dot com boom: *dot Vertigo*. Also, during this time, my HBS colleague, Steve Bradley, and I co-chaired several HBS symposia on business transformation, and published the results in our HBS Press books: *Globalization, Technology and Competition* (with Jerry Hausman), and *Sense and Respond*.[3]

During my time away from Seattle, I continued to gain additional perspective on the Puget Sound region through my son Sean. While studying computer science at Dartmouth College, Sean received a chance to spend his college off-term[4] as a Microsoft software developer working on an early Office suite, Microsoft Works.

It was exciting for Sean, having been set up with a Microsoft condo, athletic club membership, and project reviews by founder, Bill Gates. In fact it was so exciting that Sean called to tell me that he was staying at Microsoft and not coming back to finish his college degree. We then engaged in a father-son chat, and Sean did come back to finish his college degree. Afterward, Sean lost no time in hurrying back to Microsoft with his new bride to start their family. But Sean never forgave me, and a few years later surprised me with a $1 million invoice claiming that is what I owed him for his lost stock options upon returning east to finish college.

Sean's experience has become familiar to other talented professionals drawn to the Puget Sound region's magnet companies, including Boeing, Microsoft and Amazon, which helped create a high-tech industry commons. Such a commons develops in a virtuous cycle: a destination attracts talented professionals, they participate in start-up and growing companies (e.g., Nintendo in computer gaming, Amazon, Drugstore.com), and facilitates revitalizing existing companies (e.g., Nordstroms and PacCar). Other companies are drawn to the region to set up operations (e.g., Google, Getty Images), and strong university departments like the Aerospace Engineering Department, the Computer Science & Engineering Department, and the Foster School of Business at the University of Washington, which all facilitate innovation.

The university programs, in turn, attract more talented students from around the world to the region. An infrastructure tailored to the regional workforce evolves: cycling clubs, skiing clubs, and sailboat racing, and events like the annual unlimited hydroplane races during Seafair on the shores of Lake Washington. The infrastructure facilitates communication and sharing of intellectual assets as well as information on challenging job opportunities in the region. The movement of the professionals among the companies in the region accelerates diverse innovations. For example, after employees gleaned ideas in conversations with friends in research and development at Microsoft, the PACCAR Company integrated IT capabilities in its commercial trucks.

In 2003, I received a call from the dean of the University of Washington Business School offering me the new Philip M. Condit Endowed Chair. At the time, Phil was chairman and CEO of Boeing, and in our discussions about the endowed chair objectives, I was intrigued by the Boeing senior management team's 2016 strategy that was transforming the company from a "wrench-turning manufacture of airplanes" to a large-scale systems integrator that could maintain aerospace industry leadership into the twenty-first century. I was also attracted by the opportunity to chair the Boeing/UW fast track executive education program. The AIMS program was co-founded by one of my professors at the University of Washington, and has continued as one of the longest running university/Fortune 500 executive education partnerships in the country.

The dean's pitch was compelling: "What do you want to do? Spend your 24th year at HBS, or come back to Seattle to study and be involved in one of the most aggressive and innovative business transformations of the twenty-first century?"

With bike and dog in our car, Pam and I returned to Seattle, and moved into our condo overlooking the Coleman Ferry Dock, a half a block from Pike Place Market.

My relationship at HBS was a strong and special one, and I was allowed to retain my HBS chair, becoming the William Barclay Harding Emeritus Professor of Business, which also facilitated my research through financial support and maintaining close relationships with my HBS colleagues.

Upon rejoining the University of Washington faculty, I set off on a five-year research project, the Seattle Innovation Symposium (SIS) Series. Mike Eisenberg, dean of the Information School, and Ed Lazowska, the Bill and Melinda Gates Professor of Computer Science, joined me in the project.

Working with more than 100 research professors and business professionals, we produced 10 UWTV programs that continue to be broadcast on the UWTV Channel and the Research Channel:

- Creating New Billion Dollar IT-based Business in the Twenty-first Century
- IT Innovation: Investments, Process, and Results
- What Are the Key Dimensions and Issues of Team Level Innovation?
- e-Types: Innovation Strategy in a Design Firm
- Organizational Dilemma of Stewards and Creators
- Boeing: Enterprise-wide Innovator
- Working with Digital Natives
- Engaging Digital Natives in Information Technology Learning
- Digital Natives: Impacts on Management and Education
- Information Technology Leadership Learning in Action

As you can see from our SIS programs, we explored the changing environment, including the growing influence of students and workers who have grown up as digital natives. This led to an innovative business school course and a book, *Adventures of an IT Leader* (Harvard Business Press, 2009), both designed to help young managers learn the lessons of twenty-first century leadership. The protagonist is a fictionalized general manager—a composite character based on real managers in transition—who learns to be an effective chief information officer.

The SIS program provided exploratory and collaborative research for that book as well as for the related *Harder Than I Thought: Adventures of a Twenty-first Century CEO*, also published by Harvard Business Press (2013). The joint authored book follows a new CEO who transforms a contemporary airplane company by addressing the obstacles and lessons he encounters along the way.

This current book on CEO leadership extends our previous work and offers real-world academic grounding for practicing executives and those teaching leadership for future CEO's and executives.

NOTES

1. The 1955 barrel roll can be seen on: http://www.youtube.com/watch?v=WJ546BEps-M
2. William Barclay Harding was a founder of American Airlines.
3. My articles, cases, books, and videos are catalogued and available in the Harvard Business School Baker Library under Richard L. Nolan, Harvard Business School Professor. The description of my work and materials is available at the University of Washington Press website referenced under the title of this book.
4. Dartmouth required their students to attend a summer semester, and spend an off-term semester during their junior year doing an internship.

Index